CLASSICAL
STUDIES

CLASSICAL STUDIES

By

G. M. SARGEAUNT

KENNIKAT PRESS
Port Washington, N. Y./London

CLASSICAL STUDIES

First published in 1929
Reissued in 1969 by Kennikat Press
Library of Congress Catalog Card No: 79-93070
SBN 8046-0683-8

Manufactured by Taylor Publishing Company   Dallas, Texas

KENNIKAT CLASSICS SERIES

PREFATORY NOTE

OF the Essays collected together in this volume, the sixth, seventh and ninth were published in the *Hibbert Journal* ; the fourth, fifth, eighth and tenth in the *Nineteenth Century and After* ; the second, third and twelfth in the *Quarterly Review* ; the thirteenth in the *Times Literary Supplement*. I wish to make grateful acknowledgment to the editors of those periodicals for their permission to reprint them here. A few corrections and alterations have been made.

CONTENTS

1. The Eternal Wanderer   *Page* 1
2. The Greek View of Life   17
3. The Substance of Greek Tragedy   39
4. Faust and Helen of Troy   63
5. The Greek Athletic Ideal   82
6. Dance and Design in Greek Life   108
7. An Aspect of Education in Plato's 'Laws'   129
8. The Classic Pastoral and Giorgione   164
9. The Consolations of Cicero   187
10. The Landscape of Virgil   207
11. The Imperial Legend in Suetonius   226
12. Classical Myths in the National Gallery   245
13. Winckelmann in Rome   265

CLASSICAL STUDIES

THE ETERNAL WANDERER

The conception of Ulysses as the Wanderer who 'cannot rest from travel' is the invention of Dante, from whom Tennyson has taken the idea and embodied it in the romantic figure of a man for whom the purpose and joy of life lies in variety and fullness of experience, appreciated both in the actual moment of experience and in the recollection of choice moments from the past. The enchantment of exploring the unknown in the spiritual no less than the physical world possesses Tennyson's Ulysses. The hero of the *Odyssey* suffers from no delusion about the nature of sea-voyages. The desire to return to his own rocky island Ithaca is always uppermost in his mind, though he never refuses the occasion of an adventure when it is directly offered to him and his curiosity is aroused. He wanders spellbound over the sea, like the 'Flying Dutchman,' rather than of his own free will. The Sirens, Scylla and Charybdis, are adventures which he cannot avoid, foretold to him by Circe as dangers besetting the path by which alone he can return home. The long days of rowing, the fatigues of

THE ETERNAL WANDERER

battling against wind and wave, the secret hostility of unknown shores leave no room for the romantic enjoyment of strange situations. Continually the refrain occurs, ' Thence we sailed on, grieving in heart, gladly escaped from death though we had lost dear comrades,' or ' And the spirit of the men was worn by the grievous rowing.'

The attention of the Homeric Ulysses is fixed on the human interest in travelling. Whenever land is reached, the natural curiosity of the Greek shows itself in the desire to find out what kind of people inhabit that place, whether they are savage and unjust or hospitable and God-fearing. It was this curiosity and the love of profit—another pronounced characteristic of the Greeks—which involved Ulysses in his adventure with the Cyclops Polyphemus. He would not leave the cave without having seen the giant and without making an attempt to win gifts of hospitality from him. ' A safe passage and welcome gifts' is the heart's desire of this wanderer, the tale of whose adventures held the Phaeacians spell-bound, for they, like most modern readers, knew nothing of the perils and delays of the sea, since their ships ' themselves understand the thoughts and intents of men ; . . . most swiftly they traverse the gulf of the salt sea, shrouded in mist and cloud, and never do they go in fear of wreck or ruin.' In the picture of the Phaeacians is incor-

THE ETERNAL WANDERER

porated the particular ideal of men whose business and livelihood depends upon the sea, just as the life of the Olympian gods 'who live easily' is the general ideal of life for the hard-working Greeks.

The charm of travelling exists for Ulysses only in the weaving of his adventures into a tale to tell in safety by the fireside. His real feeling about the wandering life transpires through many a chance utterance. 'There is no other thing more mischievous to men than roaming; yet for their cursed belly's need men endure sore distress, to whom come wandering and tribulation and pain.' It is hunger that forces men to seek a living upon the sea. 'For this cause too the benched ships are furnished that bear mischief to foemen over the unharvested seas.' In the epithet 'unharvested' is summed up the joyless, profitless nature of the sea, for even the fish which they could draw from it was looked on as a most miserable and unwelcome form of food. It was only when 'hunger was gnawing at their belly' that Menelaus' sailors took to fishing with 'bent hooks.' Even in historical times, it is doubtful if the sea, on which by long experience the Greeks became skilful sailors, ever meant more to them than the assurance of a way home. That is the spirit in which the Ten Thousand greeted the first sight of the sea after their long retreat through the uplands of Asia Minor. It was the symbol

THE ETERNAL WANDERER

of freedom for them. And it is that idea rather than any contemplative delight in freshness of breeze or in brightness of sea and sky which gives its peculiar beauty to the ode sung by the captive women in Euripides' *Hecuba*, beginning with a cry to ' Wind, Wind of the deep sea,' with its unspoken and pathetic contrast between the freedom of the wind blowing where it listeth and the servitude of man. In the same way sunset and sunrise at sea were not emotional spectacles of beauty for them as they may be for the modern voyager, but moments which were practically useful in defining their position and the course they must steer.

' We make war in order to have peace,' wrote a Greek sage, and the difference in standpoint between the *Iliad* and the *Odyssey* is expressed in those words. The *Iliad* has always been considered artistically the finer of the two epics. The life of the warrior Achilles or Hector is splendid, but brief and austere and tragic. And yet it is surely pardonable to prefer the charm of the *Odyssey*, with its ideal of happiness for a complete life in which war is only an episode. And it is not over-fanciful to find the symbol of this widened vision of life in the smoke rising not from the captured city but from the farmsteads of his own island, which Ulysses is sick with longing to see as he waits wearily on Calypso's island. For this smoke is the sign of peace, of

THE ETERNAL WANDERER

tranquil and continuous work on the earth ; the sign of the hearth and of home-life. The thought of his home and wife is never far from Ulysses. Neither the immortality promised by Calypso nor the rich hospitality of the Phaeacians could make him forget the sweetness of Ithaca.

Knowledge of ' the cities and mind of men ' which Ulysses won by his travels did not bring with it any vague desire for far horizons. There is nothing of the restless nervous spirit of the modern traveller in his nature, no delight in the thought of far-off places still to be visited. In the eleventh book of the *Odyssey*, in the place of departed souls at the edge of the world, Ulysses inquires of the prophet Teiresias about his return, and learns that he is destined to reach Ithaca and to slay the suitors. Then the prophet tells him : ' Thereafter go thy way, taking with thee a shapen oar, till thou shalt come to such men as know not the sea, neither eat meat savoured with salt ; yea, nor have they knowledge of ships of purple cheek, nor shapen oars which serve for wings to ships. And I will give thee a most manifest token which cannot escape thee. On the day when another wayfarer shall meet thee and say that thou hast a winnowing fan on thy stout shoulder, even then make fast thy shapen oar in the earth and do goodly sacrifice to lord Poseidon and depart for home. . . . And from the sea shall thine own death come, the gentlest death that may be, which shall end thee foredone with smooth old age, and the folk shall dwell happily around thee.'[1] This prospect of more voyages into strange lands rouses no enthusiasm in his heart. His final hope is of return to his home and a peaceful death coming in some strange manner from the sea, whose influence he is destined never to dispel entirely from his life. When he narrates the prophecy to his wife it is with sadness that he says : ' We have not yet come to the issue of all our labours, but still there will be toil unmeasured, long and difficult, that I must needs bring to a full end.' And Penelope answers him : ' If indeed the gods will bring about for thee a happier old age at the last, then there is hope that thou mayst yet have an escape from evil.' In this passage, which is the final seal upon his character, we feel most clearly of all how deaf the Homeric Ulysses is to the romantic call of the unknown, looking only beyond the wanderings ordained for him to his final ordained rest and peaceful death among his own people.

Dante may have learned this legend of Ulysses' later wanderings from some Greek scholar or from a Latin version of the *Odyssey*, and have been inspired by it to write his own imaginative account of the wanderer's last voyage. But the

[1] The translations are mostly from the version by Butcher and Lang (Macmillans).

tradition of Ulysses' wanderings beyond the Straits of Gibraltar was evidently well known in antiquity. Tacitus wrote in the introduction to the *Germania* : ' Some relate that Ulysses in his long and marvellous wanderings was carried into this Ocean and reached the coast of Germany and founded and named the town of Asciburgius ; and an altar consecrated to Ulysses and his father Laertes was found there, and some monuments and tombs with Greek letters still exist on the boundaries between Germany and Rhaetia.' We know, too, that in the Middle Ages Ulysses was associated with the foundation of Lisbon under the name of Ulyssipo.

These uncertain suggestions of tradition have been drawn together by Dante to make one of the most original and dramatic digressions in the *Inferno*. In the eighth circle of Hell, Dante and Virgil witness the punishment of evil counsellors. From a bridge the poets see flames moving along the bottom of the chasm beneath them. These flames are shaped like tongues of fire, and within them are the souls of evil counsellors, for according to the words of S. James, ' the tongue is a fire . . . and setteth on fire the course of nature and it is set on fire of hell.' One of these flames which has two points contains the souls of Ulysses and Diomede, the joint contrivers of the ambush of the Trojan Horse, who achieved their ends through deceitful words. In reply to

THE ETERNAL WANDERER

a question from Virgil, ' the greater horn—that is Ulysses—of the ancient flame began to shake itself, murmuring, just like a flame that struggles with the wind,' and then quite suddenly, without any introduction, begins the narrative of his last voyage.

> Nor fondness for my son, nor reverence
> Of my old father, nor return of love
> That should have crowned Penelope with joy,
> Could overcome in me the zeal I had
> To explore the world and search the ways of life,
> Man's evil and his virtue.[1]

Dante feels that Ulysses could not have rested content within the narrow limits of Ithaca. This is the new motive introduced by him into the old legend which begins the transformation of the Homeric hero with his Greek dislike of the unlimited and unknown into the romantic adventurer of modern times. The Ulysses of the *Inferno* is no simple wanderer over the Mediterranean, seeing the cities and manners of men until the wrath of a god and the decrees of fate are satisfied—Knowledge of good and evil is the goal to be reached at the end of his travels, and the same eagerness is attributed to ' the small faithful band ' of rowers that were willing to follow him.

' O brothers,' I began, ' who to the West
Through perils without number now have reached ;

---

[1] *Inferno*, xxvi. 94 *seq*. (Cary).

THE ETERNAL WANDERER

To this the short remaining watch, that yet
Our senses have to wake, refuse not proof
Of the unpeopled world, following the track
Of Phoebus. Call to mind from whence ye spring ;
Ye were not formed to live the life of brutes,
But virtue to pursue and knowledge high.'[1]

In those lines we have no faithful image of the spirit of the Homeric Ulysses and his mariners, but the new light of the Renaissance, with its love of knowledge and discovery in all directions, as well as a reminiscence, very natural in Dante, of Aristotle's ideal, the life of speculation. The greed and curiosity of the Greek are replaced by an intellectual passion for knowledge which does not, however, weaken the love of toil and adventure. Passing through the Straits of Gibraltar, they held their course ever southwards until

                from far
Appear'd a mountain dim, loftiest methought
Of all I e'er beheld. Joy seized us straight ;
But soon to mourning changed.[2]

A whirlwind from the mountain, which was apparently the Mount of Purgatory, swooped down on them, and in a moment ship and crew sank beneath the waves.

In his poem called ' Ulysses,' Tennyson completed the transformation which Dante began. Dante conceived Ulysses as a daring explorer

[1] *Ibid.*, 112 *seq.*   [2] *Ibid.*, 133 *seq.*

THE ETERNAL WANDERER

rather than an adventurer, whose roving spirit was dominated by a definite purpose, and he devotes all his imaginative powers to describing vividly the explorer's last great voyage. Tennyson has turned Dante's explorer into a traveller of philosophic temperament, unable to rest content with what he has seen and experienced, continually and irresistibly beckoned onwards by the voice of the infinite sea of the unknown upon which the ship of man's life is launched. The setting of the poem is the classical Ithaca of the epic, where

> By this still hearth, among these barren crags,
> Matched with an aged wife, I mete and dole
> Unequal laws unto a savage race
> That hoard and sleep and feed and know not me.

But in reality the only classical quality in the poem are the adaptations and reminiscences of Homeric phrasing which Tennyson has woven into the fabric of his verse. The speaker of this dreamy soliloquy does not convince us that he has ever

> drunk delight of battle with my peers,
> Far on the ringing plains of windy Troy,

or that he could have brought his ship safely to land when

> Thro' scudding drifts the rainy Hyades
> Vext the dim sea.

THE ETERNAL WANDERER

And there is something theatrical and hollow about his order to his mariners to

> Push off and sitting well in order smite
> The sounding furrows.

This Ulysses is but the phantom of himself, a revenant, piecing together memories from some previous existence and surveying the growth of his legend through the ages in almost philosophic vein.

> I am become a name—
> I am part of all that I have met ;
> Yet all experience is an arch wherethro'
> Gleams that untravell'd world, whose margin fades
> For ever and for ever when I move.

One charm of Tennyson's poem lies in the poetic expression he has given under the name of Ulysses to the romantic temperament. He unites in concrete form all the unsatisfied needs and wishes of the modern mind reacting against the monotonous daily revolution of an elaborate material civilisation. He is imaginative and restless, unable to find happiness in the routine of work or in his immediate surroundings, enjoying everything in prospect or in retrospect even more than at the actual moment, estimating the value of life by the number and variety of his experiences. And in his son Telemachus we see the ' classical ' type of character more limited and practical in his desires and able to find happiness in the performance of the same recurring duties.

> This is my son, my own Telemachus . . .
> Most blameless is he, centred in the sphere
> Of common duties, decent not to fail
> In offices of tenderness, and pay
> Meet adoration to my household gods,
> When I am gone. He works his work, I mine.

There, in the practical Telemachus, we recognise something of the real Greek, who delighted in a world of definite tasks and purposes, and was free from any desire to 'seek a newer world,' for his confidence in the possibilities of this one had not yet failed. The Homeric Ulysses would recognise himself in such a son, but he would be sorely puzzled and distressed to hear himself described as—

> This grey spirit yearning in desire
> To follow knowledge, like a sinking star
> Beyond the utmost bound of human thought.

and to find the stubborn and mutinous rowers of his ship, who twice destroyed his hope of an early return to Ithaca, transformed into

> Souls that have toil'd, and wrought and thought
>   with me . . .
> One equal temper of heroic hearts,
> Made weak by time and fate, but strong in will
> To strive, to seek, to find, and not to yield.

The value of Tennyson's 'Ulysses' is founded securely on the life of the modern world. As knowledge increases and spreads, men see more and more of the 'unharvested' sea of experience stretching in front of them; they realise more and more acutely how much of value is slipping from them every moment; they are saddened with the thought of the brevity of their experience. In Tennyson's poem they find the perfect expression of their hopes and fears, their unspoken dreams, and they undergo in reading it the soothing influence of art. And, on the other hand, to be able to turn from the perplexing experience of our complicated society to the world of the Homeric Ulysses and 'his peers,' with its distinct horizons, its acknowledged limitations and its aversion to the problems of existence, can provide a deep source of refreshment.

All Greek art and thought is a hymn in praise of clear and limited form. The unlimited, the vague and the distant had no attractions for them, and in their list of elemental principles the Pythagoreans placed the unlimited beside evil. All through the first half of the *Odyssey* there is a contrast between the dangerous strangeness of unknown seas and lands and the sweet familiarity of the hero's home in Ithaca. And 'sweet,' not beautiful, is the epithet which Ulysses applies to his island. ' Clear-seen Ithaca, wherein is a mountain Neriton with trembling forest leaves, standing manifest to view, and many islands lie around, very near one to the other . . . a rugged isle but a good nurse of noble youths.' How lovingly are the various features of the country described, 'the long paths and the sheltering havens and the steep rocks and the trees in their bloom'; the haven of Phorcys shut in between 'two headlands of sheer cliff, where is a long-leaved olive tree and hard by is a pleasant cave and shadowy, sacred to the nymphs; and there moreover do bees hive. And there are great looms of stone whereon the nymphs weave raiment of purple stain, a marvel to behold, and therein are waters welling evermore. Two gates there are to the cave, the one set toward the north wind whereby men may go down, but the portals toward the south pertain to the gods whereby men may not enter: it is the way of the immortals.'

How well the reverence for the beauty and strangeness of Nature's work is conveyed in this oft-recurring idea that the gods have their own way of approach, their own names for mortal things. And from this haven we can follow Ulysses going ' by the rough track up the wooded country and through the heights ' to the homestead of the swineherd Eumaeus, ' in a place with wide prospect,' and from there along a rugged path to the town, past ' the fair flowing spring with a basin fashioned, whence the people of the city drew water. . . . Around it was a thicket of alders that grow by the waters all

THE ETERNAL WANDERER

circlewise, and down the cold stream fell from a rock on high.' And in the last scene, which joins in so complete a manner childhood to old age, Ulysses goes to visit his father Laertes, ' to the rich and well-ordered farmland in the upland far from the city. And he found his father alone in the terraced vineyard, digging about a plant.' And in the garden, he tells us, there were pear-trees and apple-trees and figs and fifty rows of vines promised to him as a child by Laertes, and ' each one ripened at divers times with all manner of clusters on their boughs, when the seasons of Zeus wrought mightily on them from on high.'

It is this intimacy with man and beast and soil, this desire for tranquillity in definite and clearly realised relationships of home and countryside, this recognition of the excellence of such a life that give to the *Odyssey* and the character of Ulysses their wonderful power of refreshment and delight for later and more distracted ages. The nervous irritability, the craving for incessant change, springing from over-specialised or cramped or exaggerated modes of life, were unknown to the society of that age. Yet there is nothing unsubstantial or merely idyllic about that life ; it is solid and real and convincing ; it has the assurance of elemental things. Compared with the men and women of the *Odyssey*

'Tis we who, lost in stormy visions, keep
With phantoms an unprofitable strife,

THE ETERNAL WANDERER

> And in mad trance strike with our spirit's knife
> Invulnerable nothings. We decay
> Like corpses in a charnel ; fear and grief
> Convulse us and consume us day by day.

The voyages and adventures of Ulysses drop from him in the security of his home, and, like the joy of battle, fade away into the past and become tales to while away hours by the fireside. The final and necessary slaughter of the suitors, so important in the first primitive legend, occupies a very small part in our *Odyssey*, and the stains of it are quickly swept away by the sunlight and the all-pervading sea air and the waves which beat on the rocky shore of Ithaca, 'washing away the evil of man,' according to the splendid thought of Euripides. Nothing is left to impair the happiness of the wanderer growing old in his beloved home. And who that has once become intimate with the gracious figures of Penelope and her son, with the faithful nurse Eurycleia and the swineherd Eumaeus, and has felt the ways of the sea and land of Ithaca grow dark after sunset, does not wish only that part of Teiresias' prophecy to come true which said, ' from the sea shall thine own death come, the gentlest death that may be, which shall end thee foredone with smooth old age, and the folk shall dwell happily around thee.'

THE
GREEK VIEW OF LIFE

THE 'legacy' or 'heritage' of Greece is a phrase which has been much repeated in recent years, since the traditional supremacy of the classics has been questioned and very considerably reduced in the educational system of the large English schools. Alarmed by the sudden cracks and threatened collapse of their classic temple, English and American scholars have been at pains to make the extent and value of the legacy of Greece and Rome clear to the general public, and, at times, by the excess of their fervour and protests have, perhaps, rather increased than diminished the distrust of those whom they would reassure or convert. Their theme has been, in general, the literary, artistic, and philosophical achievement of the Greeks, evident in the still existing remains, and, to a less extent, the development of their political thought and practice, and their championship of liberty.

These works constitute the actual legacy of Greece. They are in one sense the positive results of the great civilisation of Greece, and their appreciation is either æsthetic or educational, under which term is understood the study of their language and thought rather than of

THE GREEK VIEW OF LIFE

their art—though that of course cannot be entirely excluded—to train the mind in the habit of clear and precise thought. We may be delighted by the direct contemplation of her architecture or sculpture or by the artistic form of her literature whether prose or poetry, or we may benefit our minds—and this is her educational legacy in a secondary sense—by following out the recorded attempts of the Greeks to solve the various problems that arise in the course of man's social and political development, problems presented to them in a simple and fundamental form, which they viewed without any bias or tradition from earlier and alien civilisations to complicate the method of approach.

But there is another legacy which Greece has left us, more difficult to formulate, for it is negative rather than positive in result and has no place in the general estimates of their bequest to the modern world, nor is it directly presented in any of the concrete remains of that civilisation, though each fragment of literary and artistic and historical record presupposes it and assists its elucidation. It is their conception of the world and of the purpose of life in it ; or more precisely the relationship of the individual to his world. And it is the failure of their conception, showing the untenability of one of two possible attitudes towards experience, which constitutes the great spiritual legacy of Greece to the modern world, in distinction from the more visible heritage of art and literature. And when we talk of the legacy of Greece, we mean very largely the legacy of Athens, for it is at Athens in the fifth century B.C. that a Greek civilisation culminates and fails, and it is from the political and social life of that age that spring, as from a central fire, those forces of art and literature which are still active in the modern world. It is at Athens that we find the most complete and essential form of Greek civilisation, the full development of the Greek conception of the individual's relationship to the world, and it is from Athens that we draw to its full extent the legacy bequeathed to us in her failure.

In his recent book on Romanticism Mr. Lascelles Abercrombie has analysed in an interesting and illuminating manner some aspects of the romantic element in literature. He has taken as the touchstone of the romantic spirit a passage from Thomas Campbell's *Pleasures of Hope* :

> Why to yon mountain turns the musing eye
> Whose sunbright summit mingles with the sky ?
> Why do those cliffs of shadowy tint appear
> More sweet than all the landscape smiling near ?
> 'Tis distance lends enchantment to the view
> And robes the mountain in its azure hue—

and from it in particular the famous line

> 'Tis distance lends enchantment to the view,

as giving with epigrammatic force the essence of the romantic temperament, which he finally defines in prose form as being 'the habit of mind . . . that in all respects life in this world is likely to be most satisfactory when the mind withdraws from outer things and turns in upon itself.' Now, if we apply this definition of Romanticism to the great period of art and literature in fifth-century Athens we find that the element of romance is almost entirely wanting. Critics and professors of Greek literature have been at pains to detect the slightest traces of such a spirit, and though they may have discovered a few expressions and thoughts—survivals perhaps from the thought of the previous century—which may lend themselves to such an interpretation, in the main the artistic expression of that great century is singularly free from anything of the kind. Yet in subsequent centuries and elsewhere in the fifth century—if Mr. Abercrombie's interpretation of Empedocles is tenable—the vein of Romanticism is much more clear and rich, so that we are not justified in saying that it was incompatible with the Greek genius, but rather that the Greek character in its fullest and most individual manifestation, *i.e.* at Athens, found no place for the romantic attitude of mind in the development of its experience.

And, if we accept Mr. Abercrombie's concep-

THE GREEK VIEW OF LIFE

tion of Romanticism which, just because it does not dwell upon the infinite nature of the external world, is peculiarly appropriate to be applied to the Greek experience of the fifth century, it is not difficult to see why the Greeks of that age give so little sign of such a feeling in their artistic and literary remains. They were entirely absorbed in the act of living and organising their world. Distinctions between the adequacy or inadequacy of ' outer ' and ' inner things ' had not yet been made. Life ' here and now ' was the great adventure, on which they all naturally embarked, the unconscious and harmonious unity of inner and outer experience. There was no distinction between the enchanting or compelling power of what was near or distant. The distant charmed them with the hope of bringing it near to their daily lives, and that consciousness, until the first years of the Peloponnesian War had elapsed, was free from any sense of inevitable disillusionment and failure attaching to the facts of experience. Neither the records of their own past nor the rise and fall of other nations, if they had been willing to place those nations on a level with themselves, were clearly defined enough to make them feel doubtful about the issue of their own collective achievement.

The remark of the Egyptian priest to Solon, recorded in Plato's *Timæus*, that the Greeks

THE GREEK VIEW OF LIFE

always remained children is well known, and harmonises admirably with their fortunate integrity of outlook. They had the confidence in the future which children have, for the full course of experience had not yet been completed for them. They realised with supreme clearness the laws and sorrowful necessities of the individual life, and no literature has presented the facts of life, its possibilities and its realities, in clearer and more impressive form than Pindar, Herodotus, and Sophocles. But how much men might do collectively, organised in city-states and federations, and developing in the service of the state all the gifts of mind and body, this was unknown to them, and this was the great adventure of the fifth century. Before that century closed they had begun to learn in bitterness and blood that ' this world is likely to be most satisfactory when the mind withdraws from outer things and turns in upon itself.' In the literature of the close of the fifth century, and still more in the fourth and following centuries, we can trace more and more easily the beginnings of the gospel of Romanticism that ' things are not what they seem,' leading up to the refuge from a finite reality afforded by the vision of the distant mountain and the ' blue flower ' and the kingdom in the heavens.

The fortunate integrity of the Greek outlook during the greater part of the fifth century

THE GREEK VIEW OF LIFE

rested upon their sense of the past. How their past appeared to the Greeks may be gathered from the opening pages of Thucydides' history, which were written after the outbreak of the Peloponnesian War. The facts and probabilities of the past which the historian thinks worthy of admission or discussion are few, and he is quite convinced that none of the traditional legends justify the presumption that some great or extensive power existed in early times. He treats Agamemnon as a real personage, but reduces the estimate of his importance and of the heroic age in general so as to show a steady development from the insignificance of the primitive settlements to the mature power of Greece in the Periclean age. But the important moment for the Greeks themselves in their sense of the past is that they had no consciousness of social or political or artistic ideas inherited from other peoples or earlier civilisations. It may be now established that Asia Minor and Egypt exercised considerable influence on Greek artistic development, but if such surmises occurred to writers or thinkers in the fifth century they did not win serious consideration. To themselves they stood firmly on their own feet. Their world was what they had made it, and what it would be depended equally on themselves. They were a ' chosen people,' sharply conscious of the distinction between themselves and the ' barbarians,'

THE GREEK VIEW OF LIFE

whose history contained no lessons for them. There had been, to the best of their knowledge, no cycles in their history leaving a tradition of rise and fall, of advance and failure, to make them suspicious or nervous about the future. And so when the crisis of the Persian danger had been successfully passed in 480 B.C. and the Greek world had been made secure for themselves by the vigour of their own minds and bodies, the will to live and to act could realise itself under conditions of mental and physical freedom such as have fallen to the lot of no other people.

The attitude of the Greeks after the Persian wars towards experience does not show any break with earlier tradition. The general estimate of life in the sixth century B.C. is known from the poems of Solon and Theognis, and differs but little from the views of the great writers of the Periclean age. Such change as there is lies in the abandonment of any attempt to use theological suppositions to interpret experience. Æschylus really belongs to the earlier epoch, while Pindar, who lived from the sixth far into the fifth century, is in harmony of outlook with Sophocles, the artist, *par excellence*, of the greatness of Athens. Their outlook on the world might be summarised as follows. God is immortal and omnipotent, but the belief that he is in heaven did not imply for the Greeks that all was therefore well with the world. As Solon says, man must endure the gifts of the gods, meaning that good and evil alike proceed from their hands. Man's life consists in action, but the end of action is veiled in obscurity, nor is it any use expecting a sign or

> stirring of God's finger to denote
> He wills that right should have supremacy
> On earth, not wrong.

The gods are in heaven and man is on earth, and must make the best he can of the things of the earth. Courage and endurance are necessary in order to bear the sudden changes which Fate, *i.e.* the course of the world, brings about. Suffering and poverty, richness and happiness, joy and sorrow, befall men according to no calculable or revealed scheme of things. Limits are established everywhere within which man must steer his ship. 'Seek not the life of an immortal but the achievement of what is within thy power.' 'Short is the time in which the delight of man waxes, and in the same way it falls to the ground shaken by adverse doom.' 'The first of prizes is good fortune (to be comfortable), the second to be well spoken of; if a man find and possess these things he has won the highest crown.' This clear realisation of the facts of life and direct acceptance of it, without the assurance of any other help than what man can find in himself, implies sound vitality and strength of

THE GREEK VIEW OF LIFE

will. It may easily sink into listless indifference or even pessimism when physical vigour begins to fail. Of such weakness there is no trace in the Greeks of the great period. On the other hand, it is hard to overestimate the tonic effect on the Greeks, and on the Athenians in particular, of their triumph over the Persians. The will to live and act, to face the facts of life with level and fearless eyes, must have been immensely strengthened by the repulse of the forces of tyranny, and the value of life itself increased by the sudden disclosure to men sound in mind and body of a wide and fruitful field of action.

The repulse of Persia did not produce any great religious revival or new conception of the ordering of the world. The gods received thanksgiving offerings for the victory, but the honour remained with men, and that victory was not taken as a sign that henceforth the gods would interpose to make clear or smooth for man the path of life. Heaven and earth did not draw closer together, and, as before, man remained dependent on himself in the struggle for existence. But he had won more confidence in the issue of action, more hope of achieving within his narrow limits security of existence, and of realising more frequently the possible good things that life can offer. External things and actions and himself constitute his world, all the reality that concerns him, and out of that

THE GREEK VIEW OF LIFE

reality he has to shape his life. His constant effort, therefore, is towards a form of life which he is sufficient to achieve and which may be sufficient for himself as he knows himself to be. His hopes and fears are centred in this world and life.

It is an attractive suggestion, and one that has been revived in the most recent history of Greece, that the Funeral Oration spoken by Pericles in the second book of Thucydides was never delivered even in substance over the dead of any particular year in the war, but is rather a panegyric upon the spirit of Athens, and an exposition of her way of life, written by the historian when he knew that the tale of her days was accomplished, and appropriately inserted in his history before the slow demoralisation set in with the Plague and the long years of war. Twice in the course of that speech occurs the Greek word which is translated literally by 'self-sufficient.' Speaking of Athens, Pericles observes: 'We of the present generation have made our city in all respects most self-sufficient to meet the demands of peace or war'; and a little later, of the individual citizen: 'I think that each one of us is sufficient in himself to meet the most varied circumstances of life readily and gracefully.' [1]

Self-sufficiency in this double application is the ideal of Athens in the Periclean age. It is the

[1] Trans. Marchant, *Thucydides*, II. Macmillan.

THE GREEK VIEW OF LIFE

idea of a society founded on the reality of 'here and now,' where the state has achieved some sort of security for the individual, and the individual in his turn pledges himself quite naturally to live and die to uphold the state. There is no division of reality in this position; no contrast of the state with any more desirable or durable kingdom set up in the heavens; no division between the mortal life and body of the individual and his immortal soul. His pleasures and amusements, no less than his life and his daily bread, are most vividly felt to depend upon the self-sufficiency of his city. Separated from the fabric of the city, the individual wanders off into the indefinite extension of the natural world, and feels himself to be without form and void.

This belief that life in Athens could satisfy the individual rested upon one great assumption that, both in the larger sphere of political action and in the lesser one of private affairs, more must not be expected of life than a fairly equal distribution of success and failure, of good and bad things, while very often the bad will preponderate. In the brief passage of consolation towards the end of the Funeral Oration, Pericles says: 'You know amid what changes and chances you have lived; that they may be called fortunate to whose lot has fallen an honourable grief like your grief, or an honourable death like their death, and *in whose life*

THE GREEK VIEW OF LIFE

prosperity and adversity have been equally balanced.'[1] The weakness of man, the burden of his sorrows and labours, is a recurrent theme in Greek literature from the earliest times, rising at moments into the cry that it were far better not to be born at all. Year by year at the performances of the great Dionysia the Athenians were confronted with the tragic aspect of life, and Pericles is only reminding them once more of facts which, perhaps, years of peace and prosperity had made them forget. During the fifty years since the defeat of Persia, war and peace, victories and defeats, had followed each other in swift succession, and even the great disaster in Egypt had not materially hindered the general activity of Athens. Though her power on the mainland was severely restricted by the peace made by the Greek states in 445 B.C., the size and efficiency of her navy and the resources of her treasury remained as the tokens of past success and the pledge of future hopes. The course of the world had not been too hard for them. A preponderance of good things had fallen to them more than could be legitimately expected by men trained in the austere laws of life which Greek tradition affirmed. That god-given splendour which alone, according to Pindar, makes life delightful fell upon Athens not infrequently during those years, and may well have made

[1] Marchant, *op. cit.*

that generation accept the experience of 'here and now' as something ultimately real and good, whose value their artists expressed in the great works on the Acropolis.

Even to those who are familiar with the artistic and historical development of Athens, there is always an element of surprise that the actual creation of the Parthenon and its sculpture belongs to the period after 447 B.C., when a generation, which had not fought either at Marathon or Salamis, had grown up. That art gave visible form to the highest conceptions of the generations who had achieved with the devotion of service the greatness of Athens, when at last the moment came for them to rebuild the temples of their gods. Their problem was to honour and delight the patron goddess of their city with a house and statue worthy of her. And in the Parthenon and the sculpture belonging to it they solved the problem, without the use of any unknown quantity, so simply and so completely as to admit of no further improvements or refinements.

For the significance of the fifth century in Athens lies in this, that for a brief period there actually existed a form of social and political life, an organised city-state, in which all aspects of mind and body were developed and satisfied, erected simply upon the basis of the recognised limits and facts of life. There was no deliberate shutting of the eye to other possibilities experienced in the past, no concealed belief that the task on which they were engaged would never be accomplished on earth. The record of the past and their own untarnished vitality urged them forward, not in conscious pursuit of an ideal, but to the exploitation of life within the limits assigned to mortality. No vision of different or spiritual modes of life dimmed or distorted their view of the actual, or reduced the expansive force of their practical energies. Concrete existence ' here and now ' was their ultimate reality, and immortality, or rather changelessness of physical life for each god at an appropriate age, was the single but insuperable distinction between gods and men. And in the timelessness of artistic existence this distinction also vanishes, and before the sculptures of the Parthenon the Athenians could have repeated in perfect truth the words of Pindar : ' One race is there of men and gods and from one mother we both draw our breath ; yet our strength is altogether different, for men are as nothing, but the brazen heaven abides for ever, a sure habitation ; yet we have some likeness to the form or mighty mind of the immortals, although we do not know what course Fate has drawn for us to follow by day or in the night season.' [1]

For as according to the Jewish account God

[1] *Nemean*, VI.

THE GREEK VIEW OF LIFE

created man in his own image, so it may be said that the Greeks created their gods in the image of man not only in written but in visible form, and showed the value they set upon life. The art of the Periclean age, whether it presents gods or men, presents them in complete harmony of body and mind without the slightest trace of nervousness about the goodness or the meaning of life. There is no sign of trouble or doubt, no sense of withdrawal into themselves or renouncement of the external world to be seen on their faces. Nor, on the other hand, is there any suggestion of inertness or blindness to reality; the eyes of gods and men look forth openly and courageously upon their world. The Apollo at Olympia and the men and youths and maidens on the frieze of the Parthenon are intent upon the action of the particular moment without reservation or criticism, nor can we detect in their serenity the mental effort of having to conquer fears or doubts born of disillusionment.

The gods and men of the Parthenon are no less masters over life than the heroes and heroines of Sophocles' plays. In order to solace the feelings of pity and fear aroused by the course of the world, the dramatist presents in his tragedies men and women involved in, yet manifestly able to endure, and to triumph over, the circumstances of life. In sculpture their artists produced figures whose great seriousness implied

THE GREEK VIEW OF LIFE

full consciousness of the meaning of life, and raised them far above the easy sensual life of the Homeric Olympians. Those figures express the reality of the world as it is conceived by a vigorous people building their own house of life, unhampered by ideals or ruins from the past. Their belief in the desirability of life triumphs over the misfortunes and weaknesses of individual lives. 'Sorrow and joy come round to all as the Bear moves in his circling path.' But the balance of life accepted under such conditions is no less delicate than the refinements of the art which springs from it, and when the force of adversity swept too long and strongly in one direction [1] men found that reality was after all too strong for them, and that they could no longer face it with unaided courage.

The peculiar nature of the Greek view of life can be best understood in the Parthenon. The Parthenon is the perfect realisation in artistic form of that belief in necessary limits in the practical world upon which the life of Periclean Athens rested. As the city-state of the Funeral Oration claimed to assure the possibilities of life more completely than any other form of state, so in the Parthenon the artist, working with far more complete control over his material, has evolved a form able to satisfy completely the eye and mind of the spectator of like nature with

[1] In the Peloponnesian War, 431-404.

himself, by the clear articulation and co-ordination and perfect reasonableness of its structure. There, in a form into which no element of the unknown or infinite intruded, whose limits were defined and imposed by itself, the mind recognised something entirely good and fair, in which it could rest satisfied, freed from the accidents and incalculable forces by which actual life was disturbed. The Parthenon is supreme in beauty and divinity for those whose final reality lies within the limits of this life, whose ' delights are with the sons of men.' It is pre-eminently the house built with hands. There are no places in this house of God where sight is swallowed up in mystery and the eye follows soaring lines into dimness or is overpowered by space and light beneath great domes. The visitor to the Parthenon cannot fail to realise the limiting power, the strong downward thrust, the negation of all soaring to the infinite which the architrave, metopes and cornice of a Doric temple exercise. No one has expressed the sense of mystery in modern building, so different from the Greek attitude, better than Wordsworth, who speaks of the builder of King's College Chapel in Cambridge as

> the man who fashioned for the sense
> These lofty pillars, spread that branching roof
> Self-poised, and scooped into ten thousand cells,
> Where light and shade repose, where music dwells

THE GREEK VIEW OF LIFE

> Lingering—and wandering on as loth to die ;
> Like thoughts whose very sweetness yieldeth proof
> That they were born for immortality—

and of St. Paul's :

> That younger Pile whose sky-like dome
> Hath typified by reach of daring art
> Infinity's embrace.

Everywhere in Europe, except on the Acropolis, the great buildings fall short of perfection. Cathedral is contrasted with cathedral, inferiorities and superiorities are admitted ; here a west front, there the loftiness of nave or chancel, is held to be unsurpassed. But no competent critic has ever felt justified in censuring this or that detail in the Parthenon as faulty, or in maintaining that a wider front or a thicker or more slender column would have made it more perfect. Renan relates in his *Souvenirs* that he came to Athens convinced that perfection does not belong to this world and averse to believe in the miraculous. On the Acropolis he was overwhelmed by ' le miracle Grec. L'impression que me fit Athènes est de beaucoup la plus forte que j'aie jamais ressentie. Il y a un lieu où la perfection existe ; il n'y en a pas deux : c'est celui-là. . . . C'était l'idéal cristallisé en marbre pentélique.' But to the contemporary Greeks the Parthenon was no miracle. The architects and masons and workmen knew very well the relationship of each part and detail to the whole, and how each stone had come into its proper place. They had complete control over the marble in which they worked, and what could not be realised entirely in the less plastic material of human nature exposed to incalculable influences, was realised exactly in their art. The result corresponded with their intentions, because those intentions were completely reasonable and limited. The Parthenon seems a miracle—and that only in an equivocal sense—to those whose reality is no longer the forms of finite existence but a spiritual and infinite God whose power and presence they are ever striving to express in visible and therefore limited form, and so there arises that contradiction and inadequacy in expression which is nearly always felt in European art since the fifth century B.C.

It is only by comparison with subsequent works that the perfection of the Parthenon is acknowledged, and with that acknowledgment came the certainty that one form of the world, as Hegel would say, had grown old. As the Parthenon is the perfection of limited form in architecture, so it marks the point where the finite ceases to satisfy the spirit of man. In the art of the following century we notice the presence of new qualities, pathos and aloofness of expression suggesting the insufficiency of life, the effort to impress by what is vast and elaborate.

THE GREEK VIEW OF LIFE

Man is beginning to retire into himself, to withdraw from contact with the rough facts of 'here and now,' to find enchantment in what is distant in the outer world or unexplored within himself. How romantic, how disdainful of the finite is Plato's philosopher-king, 'the spectator of all time and of all being'! The fourth century, and still more the third, are full of voices crying in the wilderness, for the attempt to live according to the facts of experience had failed and man was searching for a new way of life. The romantic consciousness with its unceasing quest of the infinite had been born from the perfection and the ruins of Periclean Athens.

We might call the Athenian way of life in the fifth century B.C. the gospel of the finite. The Athenians followed out that gospel with a seriousness and energy of which the splendour of their manifold achievements is the measure. Its failure has proved that the finite is not enough for man to live by. Like Cleopatra he has discovered 'immortal longings' in his consciousness. And the full understanding of that gospel, and of all that is implied in its failure, is perhaps of more importance than the appreciation of Greek literature and art to a world which, after the reaction from the endless dreariness of Roman materialism has spent itself, now stands painfully distracted between the claims of the finite and the infinite. It is hard, at times, in

THE GREEK VIEW OF LIFE

view of the political, social, and religious controversies of the present day, to believe that we are in earnest about either the infinite or the finite. Yet it is upon the resolution or synthesis in some higher form of those two elements in our consciousness that the real progress and happiness of the Western races depend.

THE SUBSTANCE OF GREEK TRAGEDY

FIRE and Time's 'injurious hand' have spared for our consideration a very minute part of the mass of Greek literary criticism. The great centuries of Greece were singularly free from any theorising about the principles or meaning of art and literature, for the artist was the humble and unquestioning servant of the state, active at the great public festivals or in the adornment and building of the city's temples or on occasions of social union and enjoyment. It was only when the vitality of the city-state began to fail in the fourth century B.C. and disintegrating forces made themselves painfully evident in public life that Plato accused art of being one of those forces and preached the necessity of putting it in leading-strings. The fourth century was the first to hear the deceptive and distracting message of art for art's sake, with all its isolating influence on the individual, and to witness the detachment of literature and sculpture from the service of the state, and their transformation into a grace or solace of private life. The Middle Comedy and the sculpture of Praxiteles mark the first stage in that journey by which art passed from being the common enjoyment of the whole people in national theatre or temple into the secret delight of the solitary reader or the private collector. Art might still serve to adorn temples and amuse a public gathered in the theatre of Dionysus, but the dignity of solemn and serious feeling, which sprang from its union with the life of the state and religion, had for ever passed away.

In that ample outpouring of a life's experience and reflection known as the Laws, Plato is still buoyed up with the thought that the small city-state is a possibility in Greek politics. While he was writing, the power of Macedon was already established and threatening Greece in unmistakable fashion. And Aristotle, who died little more than twenty years after Plato, still clings to the outworn forms of Greek political life, summarising the achievements of the past for the instruction of future generations. And as in the great philosophical treatises he traces the development of the Hellenic mind in ethics and politics and metaphysics, so in the *Poetics* he reflects upon the course of drama and formulates certain rules and practices which the dramatist and tragedian in particular—for we no longer have his criticism of comedy—must observe if his work is to be successful. Even if the thought came to him that Greek tragedy had attained the true fullness of growth, he gives no sign of recognising that it was already moribund, and that even in his own lifetime and

THE SUBSTANCE OF GREEK TRAGEDY

for some time before, the plays publicly performed at Athens were either bloodless creatures formed of artificial rhetoric, or tragedies from the great past galvanised for a moment by the art of the theatre into a second life.

Brief and fragmentary as Aristotle's book on poetry is, it is the only piece of criticism on a definite form of art which has come down to us from antiquity, composed by one who had spoken with men who had seen and known something of the greatness of Athens in the fifth century B.C. Dionysius, Demetrius, and the author of the treatise on the Sublime are separated by centuries from the works which they discuss. Literary criticism had become a business in itself, and the feeling for the relationship of literature and life was hardly present to their minds. They concentrate too much on the verbal or formal perfection of the Greek writers, and break up that original unity of life and art which is the precious and unique quality of the creative artistic spirit in the fifth century B.C.

The preservation of Aristotle's criticism on any particular form of art is a piece of good fortune, and our sense of that good fortune is tremendously increased when the object of his criticism is Greek tragedy. For tragedy which has attained such an astonishing position in European literature is the peculiar creation of the Greeks. Epic and lyric poetry are found

THE SUBSTANCE OF GREEK TRAGEDY

in the writings of the East. Architecture and sculpture achieved magnificent form long before the golden age of Athens. Tragic drama seems the distinctive flower of the Greek genius into which all their other literary forms were gathered together, so that it contains the splendours of epic narrative and the varying moods of lyric inspiration, blended into a vaster and deeper harmony than any one of those forms could achieve by themselves, the symphonic poem of life. After the repulse of Persia from Greece in 479 B.C., tragedy becomes the supreme form of literary art in Athens. He who reads the plays of Sophocles can hardly avoid feeling how natural it is that the youthful energy and lyric flights of an earlier and youthful age should pass away into this form of mature summer beauty. Tragedy is the final experience of life as something serious. Epic and lyric poetry may be conscious of that seriousness, but they are concerned chiefly with the slighter and more transient experiences of life, which are obscured or pass away with the years.

Tradition relates that Aristotle wrote the *Politics* after a preliminary study of a hundred and fifty-eight constitutions. How many tragedies he had seen or read before writing the *Poetics* it is impossible to conjecture. During his long residence in Athens he must have seen a very large number performed and have supplemented that experience by reading. We know that the three great tragedians wrote over three hundred dramas in all, and when we recall the many other writers of the fifth and fourth centuries, some of them most prolific—Astydamas, for instance, is credited with two hundred and forty plays—the full roll of tragedies must have been immense, more than any critic, however voracious his appetite, could possibly digest. If his reading was extensive, Aristotle makes no parade of it in the *Poetics*. In addition to Æschylus, Sophocles, and Euripides, he mentions by name seven or eight other dramatists and about a dozen plays by the great Three which are no longer extant. And in harmony with this simple list of references and quotations is the simplicity of dramatic principle and structure which his criticism brings to light and approves as the most successful. Indeed, so simple are his requirements for a good tragedy that it is hard to avoid the surmise that Attic tragedy, except in the hands of a very great master, must have been a barren and uninteresting flat, the rehearsal with monotonous reiteration of an oppressive theme.

In reading the *Poetics*, it is well to remember that Aristotle's purpose in writing is not only to set the criticism of tragedy on a sound basis, but also to help dramatic poets to write successful tragedies. Frequent references to Sophocles's *Œdipus Tyrannus* make it certain that he regarded that work as a model tragedy, and the general tenor of his criticism shows that he felt Euripides at his best to be a more ' tragic ' but a less artistic dramatist than Sophocles. Modern criticism agrees with his estimate of Euripides, taking ' tragic ' in the sense of ' pathetic,' but finds it much harder to understand the scarcity and frigidity of his references to Æschylus. Aristotle seems to have regarded Æschylus in much the same manner as many critics in the nineteenth century regarded the so-called ' primitives ' in Italian painting as being incomplete but necessary stages towards the midday splendour of sixteenth-century painting. No critic can free himself altogether from the general ideas and prejudices of his own day. The language, the long-drawn choric songs, and the superhuman and portentous elements in the Æschylean drama were as alien from the spirit of the fourth century as the poetry of Keats was from the minds of the Edinburgh reviewers ; while dramatically the lack of action and absence of plot—the touchstone of dramatic success in Aristotle's view—would make him relegate Æschylus to the position, which he seems to occupy in the *Poetics*, of an important innovator and pioneer in the development of tragedy. Strictly speaking, the magnificence of Æschylus' moral and religious ideas, the splendours of his imagination, may be said to fall outside the limits of æsthetic analysis which Aristotle has imposed upon himself, but it is hard to avoid the feeling that here again the real reason of the omission lies in the insensibility of the fourth century, in which Aristotle too shared to some extent, to that grandeur of vision from which Æschylus' tragedies proceed.

Nothing could be simpler or more comprehensive than Aristotle's definition of tragedy in the sixth chapter of the *Poetics*. It is the ' representation of an action that is heroic, complete, and of a certain magnitude—by means of language enriched with all kinds of ornament, each used separately in the different parts of the play ; it represents men in action and does not use narrative, and through pity and fear it effects relief to these and similar emotions.'[1] This definition includes, without any pressing or stretching of its terms, dramas as different in form and spirit as the *Supplices* of Æschylus, the *Œdipus Tyrannus* and *Philoctetes* of Sophocles, and those late plays of Euripides in which the heroic and serious atmosphere is properly maintained. Yet the explanations and amplifications which Aristotle gives in later chapters contradict the practice of the earlier age. His advocacy of the unhappy ending does not rest upon the Sophoclean form of tragedy, and his insistence upon

[1] Aristotle, *Poetics*. Translated by W. H. Fyfe. Loeb Classical Series. Heinemann.

the great importance of a well-constructed plot means something very different from the grandiose movement of an Æschylean trilogy. It would seem as though his definition was based upon the drama of the fifth century, while his more detailed criticism took into account only fourth-century and contemporary work, when the love of classification and sharply defined types had invaded the world of literature, and the development of the Aristophanic comedy into the more sedate comedy of manners had compelled tragedy to take as its distinguishing mark a theme with an unhappy ending. It seems quite possible that the *Rhesus* affords an admirable example of a tragedy from the fourth century, satisfying the formal principles which Aristotle lays down for the dramatists of his own day. It has a well-constructed plot ending in disaster, and by its weakness in the study of character it agrees with the criticism which he makes on the tragedies ' of our younger men.' It is correct in construction but exceedingly frigid and devoid of emotional power.

Athenæus records a remark of Æschylus that his plays were slices from the great banquet of Homer, and we might say in turn that the tragedies of the fifth century are slices from the great banquet of life, invested with heroic dignity and presented as a unity. The action may end in disaster or death, or it may pass through suffering to final happiness. The trilogies of Æschylus move in a vast progression through sorrow to reconciliation. Of the seven surviving plays of Sophocles three end in happiness or reconciliation, for the *Œdipus Coloneus*, with its mysterious translation of Œdipus in extreme old age, can hardly be said to end in unhappiness. The tears which Antigone and Ismene shed are natural. The common feature of all that drama is its seriousness, its unity and isolation of action, and the presence of sorrow and suffering experienced by the characters as the result of their actions. It is those actions giving rise to sorrow and suffering which cause the spectators to thrill with pity and fear. And here we pass to the final sentence of Aristotle's definition which has caused such endless and unprofitable discussion. A tragedy represents men acting and suffering and perhaps dying, though suffering alone is enough to rouse those emotions of pity for undeserved misfortune and fear, for men like ourselves, which the successful tragedy excites. In that remark Aristotle implies the identity or the consubstantiality of the life which actors represent with that of the audience. It is a life that differs in degree but not in kind, following the same laws and rhythm as that of ordinary humanity.

We can most easily realise all that is implied in this unity of the substance of dramatic and ordinary life if we consider the relationship of an Elizabethan or a modern audience to a play of Shakespeare. No one would impugn the truth of Shakespeare's representation of the facts of life. The life which he depicts does not differ in any essential manner from that of tragedy in the fifth century B.C., though his form of it is more complicated in plot and in variety of character. But the audience feel and believe that there are other values and forces active in life of which Shakespeare takes no account. The spiritual and religious consciousness cannot be refused its right of interpretation, and though the spectator feels that the dramatist presents the facts of life as they are by themselves, with convincing truth, he knows that that is not all, and that there are other things in heaven and earth by which he can interpret the sorrows of existence. Those values and beliefs, which Shakespeare disregards in the interests of his mode of dramatic presentation, may be for the spectator the most important or precious facts in life. Shakespearean tragedy has become an artistic spectacle taking place in a world of the artist's making, which cuts the world of daily experience but is not concentric with it. Tragedy in the fifth century B.C. is concentric with life in its purposes and limitations and beliefs, and though it represents themes from a distant heroic past, the continuity of that past with the spectator's present, and its significance for him, is accepted without question.

THE SUBSTANCE OF GREEK TRAGEDY

But though there is this fundamental similarity of 'tragic' and ordinary life in the fifth century B.C., it is a similarity with a difference. The difference comes from a plot taken from the heroic life of the sacred past, from the strangeness of the costume and utterance of the characters, from their heightened capacity to act and suffer, from the employment of dance and song. The peculiar pleasure of tragedy must reside in this union of similarity with difference, for otherwise it is hard to understand why a people should ever have come to enjoy seeing represented on the stage the sorrows and sufferings of existence. In the final unity of a Greek tragedy we witness for once the harmonious fusion of artistic and religious influences to effect what Aristotle calls at one place 'the appropriate pleasure' of tragedy, at another 'the purgation of pity and fear,' and which we should be more inclined to call the pleasure arising from a sense of reconciliation with life, based upon a larger and clearer vision of things.

In a recent essay on Tragedy [1] Mr. Lucas, following Bywater and other commentators, takes the *katharsis* of Aristotle's definition in a medical sense as purgation or discharge of what is in excess. The purpose of a medical purgation is to drive out an excess of offending matter in the system and to re-establish the normal

[1] *Tragedy*, F. L. Lucas. Hogarth Press, 1928.

healthy activity of the body. The result is felt not as a pleasure localised in any particular part of the body, but as a general sense of well-being and health. Similarly the kathartic effect of the tragic spectacle is to purge the emotions of fear and pity, not to remove them altogether, but to reduce them so much as will restore the normal emotional equilibrium and give that steadiness and security of nerve, that harmony of body and soul, which are necessary for the successful conduct of life. The effect is felt both in the theatre and afterwards as a renewal and confirmation of the individual's will to live and act and face the trials and bitternesses of ordinary life. To use another medical metaphor, the tragic spectacle worked on the audience like a tonic, reviving their belief in the value of life.

This purgative or tonic effect of tragedy depends on much more than a deft arrangement of piteous and fearful incidents. Aristotle insists so strongly on the primary importance of plot that one feels at times that his ideal tragedy might be little more than a well-concocted melodrama. A careful reading of his complete definition precludes such an interpretation, though the condensed form in which he has expressed himself, the brevity of his comment on some points, or his silence on what may have seemed too obvious to need comment, render it very liable to distortion or misunderstanding. Much else beside a good plot went to produce the final effect of tragedy. Firstly, there was the tremendous spectacular power, the impact of tragedy after tragedy with its tale of pity and fear falling upon the spectator's eye and mind. Then there was the poetic or æsthetic influence, the element of beauty in it, built up by song and dance and language, the orderly spacing of the dramatist's design, into which were woven the solemn influences of heroic legend and religion, so that, under the spell of this art, the spectator accepted with joy amid his grief the tragic facts of the world.

Such things must be. The artist proves himself by his powers of selection and omission, and, as he works, the trivial and irrelevant vanish from his theme, and the substance of life seems to fall easily and naturally into clear and inevitable form. The beginning, the middle, and the end of the action are bound together by an inner necessity. Bad fortune may pass away into happiness ; prosperity may decline into suffering or death. Such things must be. Greek tragedy does not attempt to resolve the mystery of suffering. It rests upon it as an ultimate fact ; it does not point towards any happy consummation of things for which creation now travails ; it shows the tireless activity of man, his struggle for happiness and goodness ; it teaches the necessity of misfortune and suffering and death, and still more the higher necessity to endure such things rather than to give way to what is worse. 'Woe, woe, but may the good prevail,' is the refrain of the chorus in the *Agamemnon* ; it is also the keynote of all Greek tragedy and of life.

Into the question why men enjoy seeing tragedies represented on the stage, Aristotle does not enter very closely. He contents himself with saying that men have a natural love of seeing things represented, even what is unpleasant or distressing in actual life. The attraction of tragedy is the pleasure derived from seeing represented on the stage an action which arouses feelings of pity and fear. He does not attempt to go behind this curious phenomenon, which he held no doubt to be sufficiently established by the history of the Athenian stage. Nor does he say that the pleasure derived from the spectacle of tragedy was consciously felt by the audience as a purgation of their emotions of pity and fear. What the philosopher expressed in the technical language of the critic as the purgation of pity and fear was no doubt felt by the mass of spectators as a strong but indefinable emotional effect, perhaps a vague satisfaction compounded of edification and relief, in which it would not be easy for them to separate the religious and artistic influences of the spec-

THE SUBSTANCE OF GREEK TRAGEDY

tacle. The great Dionysia was not simply a dramatic competition. It was a social and religious festival. It was a yearly celebration in which the whole people took part and possessed the mysterious and impressive power of such ceremonies. In the tragic drama created by Æschylus and Sophocles they found the simplest and profoundest and most enthralling of all spectacles. The simple fundamental facts of life are the theme of that drama : action entailing happiness and unhappiness, suffering and sorrow, and joy and death. Yet here we are at once forced to ask the further question, Why did they prefer the spectacle of sorrow and tragedy to that of gaiety or comedy ? Partly because religious tradition had secured the priority of tragedy, but also because their ordinary conception of life was essentially tragic. The rhythm of life in the tragedies of Æschylus and Sophocles is the same as that in the world of daily experience.

In one of the fragments of his poetry Archilochus encourages himself with these words : ' Take delight in what is delightful, and do not chafe too much at misfortune. Recognise the nature of the rhythm which sways man's life.' The phrase is a striking one, and sums up briefly that view of life which recurs constantly in Greek literature and is expressed most typically in Theognis, Pindar, and Herodotus, who, writing at different times and for different audiences, coincide in their conception of life. Theognis addresses his friend thus : 'Endure in misfortune since thou hast joy of good things when fate came upon thee to have those things. As thou hast received evil after good so now pray to the gods and seek to escape from it.' And again : 'Danger lies in wait upon every action, and no man knows at the beginning of a deed where it will end.' 'No man can obtain all that he desires, for the barriers of grievous helplessness restrain him.' And Pindar in his grand hierophantic manner : 'Up and down the hopes of men are tossed as they cleave the waves of baffling falsity. A sure token of what shall come to pass hath never any man on the earth received from God : the divinations of things to come are blind. Many the chances that fall to men, when they look not for them, sometimes to thwart delight, yet others after battling with the surge of sorrowful pain have suddenly received for their affliction some happiness profound.'[1] And in Herodotus we read : 'There is a wheel on which the affairs of men revolve, and its movement forbids the same man always to be fortunate.' 'My wish for myself and those I love is to be now successful and now to meet with a check, thus passing through life amid alternate good and ill rather than with

[1] Pindar, *Olympians*, XII (Myers).

THE SUBSTANCE OF GREEK TRAGEDY

perpetual good fortune.' 'It is well to bear in mind that chances rule men and not men chances.' 'There never will be a man who was not liable to misfortunes from the day of his birth, and those misfortunes greater in proportion to his own greatness.' [1]

Such would seem to be the ordinary Greek conception of life. How can it be said to be tragic ? We must first of all get rid of the idea that life as tragic must end in violent death or great suffering. The practice of tragedy in the fifth century, so far as we know it, does not demand an unhappy ending. Nor does it mean that ordinary life was lived on the same serious, large, and complete scale. It means that man has a natural delight in life, and a strong spring of action in himself so that he lives and acts freely, unconstrained by the exact knowledge of his limitations. He is conscious of life as a final reality to be accepted by itself and not as part of a wider scheme of things. The same meanings and values are attached to the facts of life, for the hero on the stage and for the spectator when he has left the theatre. The curve of the tragic hero's existence may rise higher, but it starts from the same point and descends to the same point as that of the ordinary man, and rests upon the same base. And that base is composed of the simple facts of life on the earth

[1] Herodotus, I, 207 ; III, 40 ; VII, 49, 203 (Rawlinson).

THE SUBSTANCE OF GREEK TRAGEDY

as they finally arrange themselves in man's mature experience, something hard and sorrowful and precarious, whose brightness is at the best short-lived, and must fade away into old age, if it is not suddenly quenched long before by the blind stroke of death. This or something very like it is what we mean when we say that the ordinary Greek attitude to life in serious moments was tragic, and it corresponds closely with the views of life so frequently occurring in Sophocles' tragedies, which are themselves illustrated by the movement of his plays.

The citizen of a modern state, enveloped in a monotonous security by an efficient service of police and taxation and public works, comforted and assisted in a peaceful career by the inventions of science and the conveniences of civilisation, solaced by a religion which is not of this world and which finds the real life in a spiritual world within the material one, is able with difficulty to realise how exposed to occasions of fear and pity was the ordinary life of the Greeks. The safeguards and alleviations of life which we take for granted were unknown to them. Society was unstable ; the ways of life on land and sea were full of danger ; poverty and helplessness were never far away. The weakness and insufficiency of the body to win a livelihood were no less clear to them than its inevitable decay into old age and death, or its sudden collapse

THE SUBSTANCE OF GREEK TRAGEDY

from disease. Everywhere they seemed subject to circumstances or powers which were hostile and jealous. The very brilliance of the Greek achievement, the austere perfection of the artistic remains from the fifth century, help to blind us to the conditions under which their work was done. Literature from Homer onwards contains ample evidence of all that the Greeks found to fear and pity in human destiny. ' Nought feebler doth the Earth nurture than man, of all the creatures that breathe upon the face of the earth.' Theognis calls those men fools who pity the dead rather than the living, whose life and vigour pass away so quickly. Man's boasted knowledge is but delusion : his real good or woe he is unable to foresee. ' Witless are you mortals and dull to foresee your lot, whether of good or evil,' says Demeter in the Homeric Hymn. In the memorable scene after the Persian review at Abydos between Xerxes and Artabanus, who beneath their Persian names are real Greeks, Xerxes wept when he considered the brief life of the vast host gathered under his command, but Artabanus reminded him that the troubles and diseases of humanity made even that brief span intolerable. ' Envy, factions, strife, battles, and slaughters ; and last of all age claims him for her own, age dispraised, infirm, unsociable, unfriended, with whom all woe of woe abides,' and then ' the doom of

Hades ... even Death at the last.'[1] Such is the catalogue drawn up by Sophocles ending with death, the last great fear, of which we hear in the *Phædo* 'that all men except philosophers count death among the great evils, and the brave who endure it endure it only from fear of greater evils.' And in accordance with this attitude, Phædo regards it as an extraordinary thing that he did not feel pity for Socrates during the closing hours of his life. For as Aristotle remarks, 'what men find fearful in their own case, is pitiable when it happens to others.'

And yet this continual intrusion of fear and pity did not quench their spirit. There is something very wonderful about the steady nerve and balance of the Athenians during the fifth century. But this balance of spirit was not merely a happy gift of disposition. In the Funeral Oration, alluding to the religious sacrifices and festivals of the city, Pericles says that the delight we draw from these things drives away sadness, or 'melancholy,' according to Jowett's translation. To a people so occupied with making their world and living in it, so acutely conscious of the nature of human experience, so entirely dependent on themselves for power to act and endure, the spectacle of tragedy can hardly have been only an artistic or pleasurable one. The expression art for art's sake would have been

[1] Sophocles, *Oed. Col.*, 1234 (Jebb).

THE SUBSTANCE OF GREEK TRAGEDY

incomprehensible in Athens at that time, and to associate pleasure in the ordinary sense of the word with the tragedies of Æschylus or Sophocles seems like trifling with sacred things. Aristotle, when using the word 'pleasure' of the tragic effect, qualifies it with an adjective meaning 'peculiar' or 'proper.' The theme of tragedy lay much too close to the central issue of the audience's life to be regarded simply as a source of pleasure or to be observed in the detached way that a work of art demands. Greek tragedy did not aim at the presentation of this or that character or group of persons. The spectators were not meant to detect themselves in the characters on the stage or to delight in their truth to life. To think only of the hero's or heroine's character in the play, not to realise, for instance, that Creon's fortunes are as important as Antigone's in the play of Sophocles, is to fail to appreciate the significance of Greek tragedy ; for 'it is not a representation of men but of a piece of action, of life, of happiness and unhappiness, which come under the head of action, and the end aimed at is the representation not of qualities of character but of some action ; and while character makes men what they are, it is the scenes they act in that make them happy or the opposite.' [1] Happiness and unhappiness in this life is the theme of tragedy,

[1] Aristotle, *op. cit.*, c. vi. 12.

THE SUBSTANCE OF GREEK TRAGEDY

and it is the final end of action in ordinary life. Such things belong to the deepest and most serious part of man's nature, his moral and religious conscience, and their dramatic representation works on those feelings through the æsthetic sense to achieve for the Greek something similar to what such painters as Piero da Francesco and Giovanni Bellini do for the believing Christian.

The figures and scenes of those painters are solemn and inspiring, but not with the heavenly radiance and joy of Angelico's saints and angels from whom all traces of ' this muddy vesture of decay ' have vanished. The Madonnas and saints of Giovanni Bellini in particular have a full and real humanity. They are also ideal in the truest sense, ' of the world but not in it.' They have trodden the earth and know its life. They look out on the spectator with peace and power born not of innocence and seclusion from the world, but of goodness and knowledge founded on experience. The types and scenes which Bellini creates are truly heroic and saintly, in which beauty of physical form and colour is penetrated and refined by the calmness of spiritual strength. They have the power to uplift, to purge, to reconcile. In them as in the greatest Greek tragedies æsthetic and moral powers are blended together to breathe joy in the midst of sorrow, that strange state so admirably expressed in Hölderlin's couplet on Sophocles :

THE SUBSTANCE OF GREEK TRAGEDY

> Viele versuchten umsonst das Freudigste freudig
>   zu sagen.
> Hier spricht endlich es mir, hier in der Trauer,
>   sich aus.

The modern student may read or see a tragedy, or at the best the Oresteia in a day, trying to make historical imagination and antiquarian knowledge do duty for the vividness and proximity of the original spectacle. During the City Dionysia the Athenians sat for many hours on three successive days in the theatre while nine tragedies were performed. The effect of such a performance must have been overwhelming. The modern world has nothing to offer on so great a scale. The nearest approach that we can make to it are the festival performances of Wagner's *Ring* at Bayreuth. It can best be described as an immersion or saturation in the spirit of heroic life. During the performances the audience must have felt transported into a wider and grander world where they beheld the spectacle of human life with its sorrows and sufferings and death, its splendours and its eclipses, transfigured and redeemed from the narrow and broken perceptions of daily life by the artist's power and the consecration of religion. Those three days constituted for the spectator a tremendous evocation of the emotions of pity and fear. Each tragedy repeated in gigantic and solemn form not simply ' the

THE SUBSTANCE OF GREEK TRAGEDY

doubtful doom of human kind,' but the fearful and piteous tale of life raised to a power exceeding that of ordinary humanity. And it was by his absorption into the pitiful and fearful incidents of the heroic world that the spectator had his own emotions of pity and fear ' purged.' His nerve, his confidence in life, shaken by his own experience of the world, is restored or strengthened by the hero's acquiescence in, and endurance of, that tragic rhythm of life which pulsates through past and present alike.

FAUST AND HELEN OF TROY

THE creation of the Second Part of Goethe's *Faust* is separated from that of the First by a long interval of time, and though Goethe always intended to complete the drama, and was pondering its development during many years, the altered vision of wise old age, profound and suggestive but unwilling to limit itself, has made the form of the Second Part difficult to comprehend. The First Part is the drama of passion and lawless will. The Second Part is superficially a panorama, without real dramatic unity, of the experience of mature life. Instead of a plot we have variety of experience, instead of the continuity of concrete characters we have ideas and influences, typical experiences dramatically expressed in forms of astonishing reality. Faust, in virtue of the magic element in the old legend, is the thread upon which these typical experiences can be strung. He is free of time and space owing to the service of Mephistopheles, and can thus be made the receptacle for experiences of life taken from decisive epochs in the development of the western world. The beauty and wisdom and imagination of Greece, the chivalry of the Middle Ages, the art of the

FAUST AND HELEN OF TROY

Renaissance and of subsequent ages, the life of courts and camps, are presented as isolated dramatic incidents without external coherence, but absorbed and active in the stream of Faust's personality. The *dénouement* of the dramatic poem is reached not in any visible catastrophe, not even in the death of Faust, but in his admitted reconciliation with the world, which he had once cursed, that is, in his realisation that happiness is won by rational co-operation with his fellow-men.

The chief difficulty of the Second Part lies in the manner of presentation. The accepted laws of drama, the unities of time and space, the distinctions of past and present, are disregarded. In the First Part the supernatural powers of Mephistopheles are readily conceded. In the Second Part Faust himself becomes supernatural. He descends into the earth alone to bring up the images of Paris and Helen from the realm of 'The Mothers.' He wanders familiarly among the shades of the Classical Walpurgis Night and descends into Hades to beg Persephone to grant him Helen. He reappears as a Frankish knight of the thirteenth century to entertain Helen in his castle in the Peloponnese. He is carried by a cloud from Arcadia back to Germany in time to help the Emperor to victory and receive a grant of land as his reward. After such long frequenting of a world in which there are no distinctions of past and present, in which there are no separate planes of reality, the Faust of the last act, once more living prosaically in time and space, is in danger of suffering the fate of the one sober man in a company of drunkards. We are hardly prepared for this careful apologia *pro sua vita* of a centenarian, suffering the ordinary course of mortality, and founding his happiness upon the good he has already done by reclaiming waste land, and the good which future generations will continue to draw from that achievement. Judged by the mode of presentation, the transition back to the ordinary values of life seems abrupt, a dramatic bathos, a fall from the transcendental world to the common light of day. But this reclaiming of land is really only the symbol or particular illustration of the way in which Goethe held that a life might be finally harmonised, and it is our fault if we expect a highly dramatic catastrophe when the hero is a hundred years old. At the end we find all of Faust's powers concentrated on one object—he has balanced the various elements of his character; the desire of beauty is still strong, but it is now realised in the fairness of the work he is doing and in the vision of what is to be, and in his last words he pays homage to the ideal of beauty, bidding the moment of vision to stay with him because it is so fair. It is still the influence of beauty, experienced in Helen no less than in Gretchen,

FAUST AND HELEN OF TROY

which has brought him to acquiesce in the world which he had rejected and cursed in the First Part.

The conjuring up of Helen of Troy from the dead to be the mistress of Faust occurs in the earliest form of the legend. In Marlowe's *Dr. Faustus* the scene with Helen forms the climax of the play, immediately preceding the catastrophe. Faustus' attitude towards Helen is frankly material, though the beauty of the language in which Marlowe makes him express his feelings invests it for the moment with a nobler quality. Goethe has developed this episode into the principal theme of the Second Part, and invested it with a profound significance. Just as the First Part culminates in the episode of Faust and Gretchen, so the chief interest of the Second Part is the episode of Faust and Helen, not presented according to the ordinary laws of dramatic truth, but in an ideal or transcendent manner difficult to follow at first, yet finally proved most appropriate to the expression of an experience which must always be inward. Helen's marriage with Faust expresses in allegorical fashion the experience of beauty in the life of the individual. For Goethe, who constantly demanded that the individual should develop himself to the fullest extent, the experience of art was a necessary step in that development. In other ages and with different temperaments that experience

FAUST AND HELEN OF TROY

may not seem so inevitable or important, but it remains a permanent interest in civilised life, and the artistic presentation of such a theme by a poet, who was also a deep thinker and a master of practical wisdom, can hardly fail to contain moments of revelation and inspiration.

Nothing could be more natural than the way in which Faust enters upon his exploration of the world of beauty. A chance incident—the Emperor's wish that Faust, as the possessor of magical powers, should bring on the court stage the forms of Paris and Helen—is the occasion of his æsthetic conversion. Quite unsuspectingly Faust is confronted by a form of beauty and at once responds to the appeal. The exact nature of his need—hitherto felt only as a vague dissatisfaction with the emptiness of life—and the possibility of its satisfaction is borne in on him at one and the same moment. He recognises in Helen's beauty something that could give inspiration and value to the life which he was dissipating. Dressed as a priest with a wreath on his head, the outward signs of his consecration to a new ideal, he thus addresses the form of Helen :

> Have I still eyes ? Is beauty's very spring
> Full gushing to mine inmost sense revealed ?
> Most blessed gain doth my dread journey bring.
> How blank to me the world, its depths unseal'd !

FAUST AND HELEN OF TROY

> What is it since my priesthood's solemn hour !
> Enduring, firmly-based, a precious dower !
> Vanish from me of life the breathing power
> If, e'en in thought, I e'er from thee decline ! [1]

In the second act Faust begins his experience of beauty in its two principal forms, womanly beauty as a power in men's lives—a theme that was very dear to Goethe—and artistic beauty, inevitably expressed in that age under the forms of classical art. Into this world Faust is introduced not by Mephistopheles, who knows nothing of Greece, but by Homunculus, the mannikin of the alchemists, whom Dr. Wagner has opportunely produced, according to prescription, in a glass bottle. Homunculus is the most fanciful and puzzling of all Goethe's creations. We may, perhaps, see in it a personification of the over-developed imaginative intellect, able to enter into and interpret the experiences of others, but haunted by the unreality of its own one-sided existence, and eagerly seeking how it may pass into a form of life where the balance of body and spirit may be restored.

But though Faust is absent or silent during most of the Classical Walpurgis Night, the scene is closely connected with the development of his mind. It is the preparation for his meeting with Helen, the ideal of Hellenic beauty. It is

[1] Part Two, Act I, 1880 *seq.* (Swanwick).

FAUST AND HELEN OF TROY

his initiation into the world of Greek art. But he is not initiated personally. It would have been tedious for him to review all the artistic forms of the Greek imagination with which this scene teems. They are rather to be conceived as influences present, so to speak, in the air which he breathes in Greece, and absorbed by him during this wonderful timeless night before he reappears to welcome Helen's return to Greece in the next act. In its totality this scene brings before us a large number of mythological figures, progressing from the half-human—for instance, the Sphinxes—to the completely human, the lowest possessing a clear and definite nature, the highest an equal clearness of form, instinct with a ceaseless activity and lust for action and self-expression. Virility and power to impress are felt everywhere in this world, and we can see how free Goethe was from all that feeble classicism which imagines the Greek spirit to be a sentimental yearning for the creation or enjoyment of the pretty and graceful. The life and beauty of Greece at their highest development were essentially masculine and active; those Praxitelean shapes of which Shelley sang belong to the period of failing strength. Cheiron expresses the true Greek feeling in his few lines of comment about women to Faust:

> Oh, woman's beauty! empty words, I find;
> Such beauty is too oft a lifeless stick;

> The only shape that can enchant my mind
> Is one that 's vigorous, full of joy and quick ;
> Mere beauty 's lifeless, with itself content,
> By charm alone I suffer ravishment.

At the opening of the third act Helen is discovered standing in front of Menelaus' palace at Sparta, and near her are grouped the chorus, a band of captive Trojan maidens. She announces that she has just returned from Troy, and that her husband Menelaus, who is remaining on the shore to review his warriors, has sent her on in advance to prepare everything for a solemn sacrifice. Nothing, however, has been said about the victims to be offered, and Helen is troubled by the thought that she herself may be the destined sacrifice.

The first suggestion of anything peculiar in the situation comes with Helen's entry into the palace. As she mounts the steps, the palace seems to her the same, and yet not the same, as in bygone days,

> the royal house,
> Long missed, oft yearned for, well-nigh forfeited,
> Before mine eyes once more it stands, I know not how—[1]

Hardly have the chorus finished their first ode when Helen returns in evident dismay and describes the strange experience which had befallen her within. The curious foreboding

[1] *Ibid.*, Act III, 118 *seq.*

FAUST AND HELEN OF TROY

which she had felt outside the palace had been increased on her entry.

> I wondered at the drear and silent corridors.
> Fell on mine ear no sound of busy servitors,
> No stir of rapid haste, officious, met my gaze;
> Before me there appeared no maid, no stewardess,
> Who every stranger erst, with friendly greeting, hailed.
> But when I neared at length the bosom of the hearth
> There saw I, by the light of dimly smouldering fire,
> Crouched on the ground, a crone, close veiled, of stature huge,
> Not like to one asleep, but as absorbed in thought—[1]

And when Helen would pass into her bed-chamber the form sprang up,

> Barring with lordly mien my passage, she herself
> In haggard height displays with hollow eyes, blood grimed,
> An aspect weird and strange, confounding eye and thought.[2]

When this mysterious and disquieting being, whose name is Phorkyas, comes out from the palace the action is precipitated. After some curious wrangling between her and the chorus and Helen, in which Helen's unreality becomes more and more evident, Phorkyas learns that a sacrifice is to be prepared. She has little difficulty in convincing them that they are to be the victims, and induces them to follow her to

[1] *Ibid.*, 182 *seq.* [2] *Ibid.*, 201 *seq.*

a place of refuge near Sparta, where, in the absence of Menelaus, some northern invaders have established themselves in a castle of novel and magnificent architecture. Here at last the hints of earlier passages are confirmed, and it is made amply clear that Helen and the chorus are no real personages of flesh and blood ; for these northern invaders are the Frankish conquerors of the Morea, and their leader is Faust, miraculously translated from Germany to Greece and enjoying another cycle of experience.

This moment of transition from the classical to the mediæval world is a suitable point at which to pause and consider the peculiar quality of this opening scene. It is the point where the symbolic nature of the drama becomes evident. The characters cease to be concrete personalities and pass into symbols of certain ideas and influences, and the interest lies more in the expression of those influences, of which the characters are the symbols, than in the development of real individuality.

The style of the scene is exactly that of Greek tragedy. The narrative part is written in ' Alexandrines '—six-foot iambic lines. The diction is full and smooth, simple and lucid, and reproduces so closely the texture of classical tragedy that this scene might be a translation executed by a highly-gifted poet. It is, of course, quite clear that Goethe did not wish to make a simple parody of Greek drama. The quality of this scene, so equably illumined by the high light of poetry, is far removed from parody. What he has really achieved is to fix in clear form the ideas of physical and artistic beauty as he, at least, understood them to have existed for the Greeks. The former is personified in Helen, the latter in the literary composition of the scene, but as the scene advances and Helen's bodily reality appears more and more ghostly, she becomes the symbol of Greek beauty, freed by the lapse of time from all physical or material elements, possessing, like the language in which she speaks, that intangible grace of form and matter so simple and plain to see, yet so elusive to grasp. It is pre-eminently a beauty of rational form, the pleasure derived from watching the orderly development of an action or idea in which the emotions and instincts of the heart have little share. All through this opening scene the lucid exposition of facts, movement by discussion in question and answer, is the controlling principle. The tone is classical or real, in contrast with the romantic quality of the following scene, and the appreciation of such art belongs rather to the intellect than to the heart. That, at least, is the distinction which Goethe seems to have felt between the two worlds, and the appreciation of this opening scene depends upon grasping it. The development of the action is so slow, and the content, if considered apart from the form of presentation, appears dull and unimportant and remote from the sphere of our needs ; it is always concerned with the immediate facts of the situation. And that, perhaps, is exactly the feeling which Goethe intended to arouse in order to lead the way to a just criticism of the worth of classical beauty for the modern world. We can learn to enjoy it, and we can use it for the education of our taste, but we must not look upon it as sufficient for our needs. It ought not to exercise claims beyond the limits assigned to the works of the past. And there is, too, an extreme brittleness in this classical beauty ; it is so frail and delicate that even ' a summer cloud can overcome it ' ; its serenity and happiness fail on the intrusion of any hostile element, of any ugliness. This we seem to see typified in the effect which Phorkyas exercises upon Helen and the chorus. Their life fails and wilts and becomes unsubstantial in her presence. The Greek enjoyment of physical beauty was largely direct and sensuous. Helen lives in her own attractions, recalls all who have desired her with violence, has seen in them nothing but passionate lovers. There is no romantic element in her consciousness.

The more spiritual or romantic conception of beauty belongs to another age, of which Faust

FAUST AND HELEN OF TROY

is the representative in the next scene, where we find Helen and the chorus within his castle in mediæval Greece. Presently Faust enters in the rich court attire of a knight, bringing with him a man in chains, Lynceus, who as watcher upon the castle tower had failed to warn him of Helen's approach. In his defence, spoken in rhyming quatrains (a sign that we have passed beyond the form of the classical world), Lynceus pleads that he was so overcome by the vision of Helen's beauty that he forgot all his duties to his master:

> Watching for the morning, gazing
> Eastward for its rising, lo !
> On the south my vision dazing,
> Rose the sun a wondrous show.
>
> Neither earth nor heavenward turning,
> Depth nor height my vision drew ;
> Thitherward I gazed, still yearning
> Her, the peerless one, to view.[1]

Helen is no less astonished at this veneration than at the courtly and chivalrous homage paid to her by Faust and at his exaltation of herself as the supreme power in his land, expressions of sentiment so different from that of the Greeks towards women. She adapts herself, however, with perfect ease to these new conditions, and, charmed by the northern fashion of speech and rhyme, she quickly learns its art under Faust's

[1] *Ibid.*, 735 *seq.*

FAUST AND HELEN OF TROY

instruction. The scene culminates in a passage of rhyming couplets in which Faust describes himself as sunk in the vision of her beauty, while Helen is herself the spirit of beauty old yet ever new, passing from master to master, woven for the moment into Faust's being, and more true to him, the unknown one, than to those she has known in the past. The lines are famous and of singular beauty, applying not only to the dramatic situation, but passing beyond to suggest the relation of the spectator to the work of art, which dies with each generation of its lovers and is reborn with the succeeding one and is no less true to it.

In the next scene we are amid the bowers and cliffs of Arcadia. The chorus learn from Phorkyas that a son has been born to Helen and Faust. It is the miraculous child Euphorion, who soon appears in festal attire with his parents. Euphorion, rapidly growing to manhood, and more and more excited by his own inspiration, quickly tires of dancing with his parents and the chorus. He leaves them and climbs alone from point to point on the cliffs, singing with lyrical rapture, until at last, overcome by desire to enter into the world of action and to share men's sorrows and needs, he imagines he has wings to bear him away through the air; he leaps off from a pinnacle of rock, flutters for a moment in the air, and then falls like a meteor to the ground at the feet of

FAUST AND HELEN OF TROY

his parents. His body disappears, but his voice is heard summoning Helen to keep him company in the world below. She vanishes from Faust's embrace, leaving in his arms her garments, which in turn dissolve into clouds, enfold Faust, and carry him away through the air. Phorkyas lays aside her mask and veil and reveals herself to be Mephistopheles, the author and stage manager of this phantasmagoria.

In this last scene the characters have become more and more unsubstantial. Faust and Helen no longer play the leading parts; the reality of their being has passed into their son Euphorion, whom the chorus openly address as 'sacred poetry.' With his birth a new stage is reached in Faust's experience of art and beauty. No sooner has the music begun, with which his appearance is accompanied, than Phorkyas also breaks into song:

> Hark those notes so sweetly sounding,
> Cast aside your fabled lore,
> Gods in olden time abounding,—
> Let them go! their day is o'er.
>
> None will comprehend your singing;
> Nobler theme the age requires,
> From the heart must flow, up-springing,
> What to touch the heart aspires.[1]

The creation and enjoyment of art and beauty must not be cramped by the tradition of the past.

[1] *Ibid.*, 1192 *seq.*

The claims of the present are paramount, and inspiration must be sought in it so that the harmony of artist and public, founded on the common emotions of the heart, stirred by life here and now, may be established.

The chorus too, no less than Phorkyas, feel the birth of a new world, the discovery of the inner life and its poetry, a world which cannot fail in the way in which the world of classical art can be shattered by the intrusion of alien elements, when the whole edifice of reasonable and ordered reality comes crashing down. In their reply to Phorkyas, they say:

> Vanish may the sun's clear shining
> In our soul if day arise,
> In our heart we, unrepining,
> Find what the whole world denies.[1]

The Arcadian happiness of Faust and Helen has been short-lived. Euphorion, their son, the genius of modern romantic poetry, born from the communion of the mediæval with the classical spirit, cannot live in seclusion. He must break with the classical tradition which would confine him to the ancient forms and moderate his transports. There is incorporated in him a lyric endeavour to reach the ideal, as well as a delight in striving, altogether alien from the serenity of Greek art in the sixth and fifth centuries B.C., whose difference we can best measure here by

[1] *Ibid.*, 1204 *seq.*

contrasting the calm beginning of this act with the excitement of its close. Euphorion longs for the world of living men, from which to draw vitality and inspiration, instead of looking back with regret on the past and idly repeating the pleasures of appreciation.

And so Faust is not overcome by the death of Euphorion and the return of Helen to her own world of shades. He has gained knowledge of art and beauty, and that knowledge remains with him, symbolised in the garments of Helen left in his arms, a power to raise him above all common things, which he can use for consolation or delight, but by which he cannot live. A continuance of that Arcadian life, which has only been justified by the life of Euphorion, would be a state of lifelessness, of idle indulgence in art for art's sake. Faust has heard the voice of his own son calling him forth to action. Happiness and beauty, as Helen says in her last words, never dwell together for long, and even the artist is made happy, not by contemplating the beauty which he has created, but by the slow and laborious realisation in external form of his vision ; and Faust, who is not a type of artist, but of man engaged in learning the lessons of life, could no more have rested content in an artistic Arcadia than a capable and active mind could remain indefinitely in the south merely contemplating the remains of ancient Greece or Rome.

FAUST AND HELEN OF TROY

The speech with which Faust begins the fourth act is really the seal upon his experiences in the third. The forms of the world of classical beauty have entered into his mind as a permanent quality. He is alone on a mountain-top, and the clouds which brought him there are rolling away to the east. As they mingle and change their outlines he fancies that he sees in them majestic forms of beauty—Juno, Leda, and Helen. He can now speak of their loveliness with serenity of mind. Once the mere name of Helen had driven him into passionate excitement, now his will has been purified and calmed. And then another fancied shape in the clouds brings back the thought of his first love, Gretchen, whose beauty he now sees and values rightly, looking back on it with regret as possessing a spiritual quality, a moral and physical fairness and freshness denied to his more mature experiences.

This passage may be considered the epilogue to this strange and beautiful episode. A first reading must always prove a difficult task because of the strange fusion of different worlds and planes of existence. But in the work of a poet at his best—Dante is the most sublime example of this truth—nothing is past or dead. Distinctions of past and present, of what is historical or imaginative, vanish in the transforming light of poetry. *Omnia mutantur, nihil interit.* And in reading the Second Part of *Faust* it is wise to bear always in mind the words with which Goethe concluded the whole drama :

> All that is transitory
> Is but a symbol.
> Here what is incomplete
> Finds its completion ;
> What cannot be described
> Here has been realised,

for there is little difference between the Kingdom of Heaven, as the Chorus Mysticus here describe it, and the world of the artist's vision.

THE
GREEK ATHLETIC IDEAL

AFTER existing for more than 1100 years the Olympic games were abolished in A.D. 393, and from that date until the nineteenth century athletics in the Greek sense of the word may be said to have disappeared from the world. Various forms of hunting were practised by the rich nobles when they were not engaged in the sport of war, and in England, at least, during the eighteenth century horse-racing and prize-fighting were popular. But when in the nineteenth century interest in the problem of education awoke, and the public schools began to set their houses in order, the value of athletics in the form of organised games to occupy the leisure as well as to develop the physical powers of boys became apparent. The various forms of sport favoured in the schools were carried on at Oxford and Cambridge, and the pleasure and benefit derived from them gave an impulse to other games which are more possible and suitable for grown men engaged in business with only a limited amount of leisure. But the form of modern sport or athletics bears the characteristic mark of its place of origin and is sharply distinguished from the Greek practice. The essence of school sport is the competitive spirit, and while athletics in the narrow sense of the term—that is, running and jumping—have maintained their place in schools and in the larger world, the real enthusiasm for sport has centred on 'team' athletics, such as cricket and football and rowing. It is only in quite recent times that tennis and golf, where the greatest prizes fall to the 'single' player, have attained a popularity equal to that of any other game. Athletics, as the Greeks practised them, were essentially the field in which the individual could distinguish himself; there was little or no 'team' spirit, but the element of danger was not absent from them. Chariot-racing, especially with the four-horsed chariot, was very dangerous; wrestling was rough; boxing was severe; and the *pankration*, a mixture of wrestling and boxing, was even more severe from the freedom of its methods.

The various forms of modern athletics are, except on general principles, unconnected with our ordinary activities. Greek athletics were directly useful for practical purposes; for war, which was never far from the city-state of the sixth and fifth centuries B.C. and demanded fitness in all the adult male population; for travelling by land or sea, which required hardness and the ability to fight for one's life at any moment. It is perhaps their intimate connection with the rest of life which has made it possible for them to be used as a theme for literature and art, while the modern athlete lives in so ephemeral a manner in the sporting columns of newspapers, in photographs, and in the trivial gossip of personal paragraphs. We have memorable descriptions in English prose of fox-hunts and prize-fights and cricket matches, but modern sport lacks its inspired poet or sculptor to shed upon it ' the God-given splendour ' which Pindar, for instance, felt was its due.

The different forms of literary art which the Greeks perfected during the period of their creative activity have remained as permanent types upon which all subsequent European literature has been moulded, not in the superficial sense of being simple imitations of the peculiar Greek texture of style, but in the adaptation and development of those grand forms to stir our emotions. The Romans, we are told, claimed satire for themselves ; yet it is doubtful if satire has ever proved itself to be a great form of art in the manner of tragedy or epic poetry ; doubtful if it belongs to great creative epochs and is not rather a product of those periods when, as Hegel quaintly observes, ' the owl of Minerva is already on the wing and with the twilight grey paints everything in grey.' But while European literature has drawn all its modes of expression from the Greeks, there are certain modes understood only by them, instruments on which they made no less perfect music than on those which we too can handle, whose secret has perished with their creators. These forms survive to prove to us the surpassing richness and distinction of their genius. The comedies of Aristophanes and the *Odes* of Pindar on athletic victories remain unique creations in the world of art.

Pindar's life extends over the most triumphant period of Greek history. Born at Thebes in the sixth century B.C., he composed his first ode for a Thessalian noble before the battle of Marathon in 490. He was over forty when the freedom of Greece was finally won at Salamis and Platæa. He lived to see the establishment of the Athenian Empire, the ruin of his beloved Ægina, and the frustration of the Athenian bid for land power by her defeat at Coronea in 447. His last ode is generally assigned to 446, when Athens, by means of her empire and wealth, was drawing to herself all the genius of Greece. The splendid buildings on the Acropolis had been designed and begun. Sophocles was the favourite master of Greek tragedy, and the last great phase of Greek art—the Athenian phase—was beginning. The generation to which he belonged in way of life and ideals had already passed away when death came to him at Argos.

The victories which Pindar celebrates were obtained by athletes from all the important centres of Greek life in the fifth century B.C. There are the princes and rich nobles from Sicily and

Cyrene and Thessaly, athletes from Magna Græcia, from Rhodes and Ægina, the mother of so many victors, from Thebes and Opus, from Corinth and Orchomenos, from Athens and Acharnæ and Argos. Sparta is the only important place from which Pindar apparently received no commission, for Sparta had ceased to send competitors to the great games as part of her general policy of aloofness from the rest of Greece. Thus, if we except Arcadia and the other small cities of the Peloponnese, the Epinikian odes afford excellent material for estimating the general feeling not only about athletic success, but about the larger issues of life in which bodily vigour was always an important advantage. It is unlikely that Pindar, though he looked on himself as an inspired poet and preacher, the exponent of the divine wisdom of Delphi, would utter sentiments or give advice which he knew to be contrary to the accepted ideas of his audience. As teacher he may criticise existing standards of conduct or protest against wrongful views about divine beings, but as a professional poet, who was to some extent dependent materially upon his commissions, he must fall in with the views of his patrons and audience, must speak a language in which they could recognise the qualities—refined, perhaps, and glorified—which they held to be desirable. Upon this common foundation Pindar has reared a structure which the Greeks whom he addresses would recognise as expressing most perfectly their own dimly-conceived and incomplete reflections upon the way of the world.

We cannot doubt that Pindar enlarged immensely for them the significance of victory in the games. It is indeed the function of the great poet to widen as well as to deepen an individual experience and to draw into the one central light thoughts and acts which seem at a first view out of relationship with it and of small importance. That is all to the credit of the poet, fulfilling to his public the duty of teacher, as he himself understood it, according to the Greek tradition. He never regards a victory as an isolated fact in the life of the individual; it becomes symbolic of the whole of life, and through the individual is woven into the fabric of the corporate life. At the same time, he increases the field of illumination to include both the past and present, so that the victor sees the glory of his achievement in the games blend with the glory of heroic deeds, the glory of an Achilles or Peleus who strove, not for athletic success, but for a crown of honour and glory upon the whole of life.

The other great writers of the fifth century who deal with the contemporary life of Greece present it at a moment of crisis. Herodotus narrates the culminating moments of the supreme struggle against the East, Thucydides the final agony of rival ambitions in the Peloponnesian war.

Æschylus, who in time is closely contemporaneous with Pindar, debates little else in his drama except problems of theology and ethics presented on the stage of a superhuman world. Pindar remains the poet of normal life and peace, aloof from the great struggles, aloof from the science and speculation of Ionia and Athens, interested in the actual living of life, in the establishment of an ideal that can be realised, in the clear limitation of human hopes and fears. His thought is based upon the popular consciousness of Greece, which found honest but incomplete expression in the earlier poets, Hesiod and Theognis. Beneath the magnificent vesture of his language his audience detected the sentiments of their own hearts, amplified and perfected, but never passing beyond their comprehension. In the hardest of all tasks Pindar rarely fails : he is the singer of the average ideal of life ; not over-intellectualised, as in the second half of the century at Athens ; not over-burdened with military discipline, as at Sparta ; fresh to receive impressions, and no less fresh and sensible in its judgment on them ; accepting life as it actually comes with its joys and sorrows and free from all nervousness, whose form we can still admire in the marbles from Ægina and in the few precious fragments from the temple of Zeus at Olympia, the inmost shrine of the Pan-Hellenic athlete ; best of all in the torso of the Apollo—all the energy of his spare

THE GREEK ATHLETIC IDEAL

strong body gathered up into the service of the mind and flung into the gesture with which he dominates the struggle.

Pindar distinguishes three moments of importance for the competitor in the games: the time of training, the actual struggle, and the years after success. Interest in the modern athlete is largely concentrated on the first two aspects, and the adjustment of success with the rest of life is never considered. The wide sweep of Pindar's vision, belonging to the youth of Greece, as yet unconvinced by secular experience that man must be content with the 'broken arc' on earth, disdains to leave the athlete or the prince in the moment of success. Beginning and end must be harmonised with the constant facts of all experience, and the three stages in the athlete's career are shown to be typical of the three great periods of life—youth, manhood, and old age, each of them revealing only under trial its peculiar excellence: 'It is trial that maketh manifest the prime of those virtues, in which any one shall have proved himself pre-eminent, whether as a boy, a man among men, and thirdly as an elder among elders according to the several portions of life, which we, the race of men, possess.'[1] And there is one more excellence

[1] *Nemeans*, 3. 70. The translations, with a few exceptions, are taken from the very convenient edition of Pindar (text translation, etc.) by Sir J. E. Sandys in Heinemann's 'Loeb' series.

THE GREEK ATHLETIC IDEAL

without which neither the athlete nor the ordinary citizen can obtain the crown of success : it is the ability to recognise and to seize what is best in each passing occasion.

'Trial is the test of mortal man ;'[1] 'those who make no trial have an inglorious obscurity.'[2] Man's life, according to Pindar, draws all its glory from the varied forms of action, whether in the games or on behalf of his city in war or counsel ; and counsel is especially the virtue and the service of the old. Trial, toil, and danger are words which occur continually through these odes and awake in the individual the spirit of adventurous daring and endurance. 'If there be any bliss among mortal men, it doth not reveal itself without toil.'[3] And in the effort to achieve success a man must spend freely both his physical powers and his money. A good trainer is necessary : 'It is foolish not to learn betimes.'[4] A trainer, however, cannot do everything, and Pindar regards the true athletic or sporting instinct as something hereditary. No amount of professional lore and training can compensate for the absence of this spirit. 'That which cometh of Nature is ever best : but many men have striven to win fame by means of merit that cometh from mere training.'[5] This gift of Nature combines a natural aptitude for many

[1] *Olympians*, 4. 17. [2] *Isthmians*, 4. 30. [3] *Olympians*, 12. 28.
[4] *Ibid.*, 8. 60. [5] *Ibid.*, 9. 100.

THE GREEK ATHLETIC IDEAL

forms of sport, such as exists, for instance, in certain classes of English society, with the will to 'hold on' in an uphill fight and to endure, without losing cheerfulness or courage, the hard knocks which precede victory no less than defeat.

'The great adventure demands no coward soul,' cries Pelops in the first Olympian ode. 'Excellence without the love of adventure wins no honour either among men on land or on board hollow ships.'[1] So, too, the heroes long for the voyage of the *Argo*, refusing 'to nurse at home a life that is without adventure,' and in his contemporaries Pindar looks for a spirit which 'boldly essays all the exploits for noble deeds.'[2] It is toil which brings a man peace at the last. 'Out of labours undertaken with the aid of youth and right there cometh a gentle life at the approach of eld.'[3] Goodness of breeding, a daring spirit tempered by wisdom, the will to spend and be spent, these are the essentials for success in the games and equally in the arena of the city-state, and we can feel little surprise at Pindar's glorification of the games, for it springs from a sense of the immense importance of the effort after victory to the character, so that the merely physical and perishable element in the victor's crown is transfigured by ethical values.

Pindar never attempts to describe the actual struggle for victory at Olympia or elsewhere.

[1] *Olympians*, 6. 9. [2] *Pythians*, 5. 116. [3] *Nemeans*, 9. 44.

THE GREEK ATHLETIC IDEAL

He sang primarily for those who were familiar with the games, if not in all the splendour of the great gatherings at Delphi or Olympia, at all events as they were to be seen at many minor festivals throughout Greece ; and he must have felt that such descriptions, even if they could be brought within the compass of his art, were superfluous. His references to the various events are almost conventional : a few words to recall the rush of the chariots ; a reference to some characteristic throw in wrestling, ' the cunning skill that swiftly shifts its balance, but never falls,' [1] to the sweat upon limbs under a burning sun,[2] is all that he permits himself. He seems to turn deliberately from the memory of blows and physical exhaustion to recall the more ideal aspect of the scene. He re-creates the atmosphere of the games, calling to mind the landscape of each place with touches of local colour vivid enough for those who knew each spot : the grassy meadows at Cirrha where the Pythian chariot races were held, the ' shady primeval mountains ' near Nemea, the sunny hill of Cronos, and ' the grey-hued adornment of the olive spray ' at Olympia. He dwells with delight upon the beauty of those familiar scenes, most lovely when after sunset ' the moon with her car of gold had at eventide kindled the full orb of her light,' [3] and the evening banquet takes place amid the

[1] *Olympians*, 9. 91. [2] *Nemeans*, 7. 73. [3] *Olympians*, 3. 19.

flashing of torches in the spot set apart for it by Heracles at Olympia, and 'in the joyous festival all the precinct rang with song like banquet music.'[1]

He brings back the proud moment of victory when 'all the friendly host raised a mighty cheer,' and with the characteristic Greek feeling for physical beauty recalls the impression produced by the mingled fairness and strength of some victorious athlete like the son of Archestratus 'whom I saw winning victory with the might of his hands—one who was fair to look upon and was graced with that bloom which, in olden days, by the blessing of Aphrodite, warded from Ganymede a ruthless fate.'[2] The adjective by which Pindar expresses the form and strength of the athlete and the spectator's appreciation of it means literally 'what is gazed at or admired' ($\theta a \eta \tau \acute{o}\varsigma$). He uses it of anything which by its beauty can hold the eye spellbound: of the temple of Apollo at Delphi, of the morning star, of the limbs and of the human body seen at the games, so beautiful that the women, 'each, after their kind, have in silence prayed that they might have such a one for their dear husband or son.'[3] Not the straining of muscle and nerve, which would remain lively enough for a while in the memory, but the moments of beauty and glory are selected for the more lasting benediction of poetry, moments which may follow the victor into

[1] *Olympians*, 10. 76. [2] *Ibid.*, 10. 100. [3] *Pythians*, 9. 98.

THE GREEK ATHLETIC IDEAL

his old age and which may make the ode full of the spell of beauty for those who read it in after-time.

'Very strong is he and fair of form, and he has excellence not at all inferior to his frame.'[1] Beauty of form is to be the visible sign of inward excellence (ἀρετή), that peculiar and comprehensive word in which is contained for Pindar all the qualities desirable in man. It embraces courage and strength of will, the desire to achieve glory and to fulfil perfectly one's duty towards the gods and one's own city-state. The possessor of this excellence is, within the limitations of Greek morality, the perfect gentleman, the perfect warrior, who can weave together strength and daring and knowledge, so that when the occasion comes he is true to himself and can seize it with promptness first in the games and then in the larger arena of life. 'Success is the crown of perfect glory,'[2] but victory in the games is an early event in life, is but the 'bright porch' of the building which is to be erected, and Pindar never lets his athlete depart without counsel and good wishes for the future.

It is impossible to read carefully through these triumphal odes without noticing the constant recurrence of the word 'grace,' either in direct appeal to the three Graces, or in words derived from their common appellation or from their individual names, Aglaia, Thalia, and Euph-

[1] *Isthmians*, 7. 22.   [2] *Nemeans*, 1. 10.

THE GREEK ATHLETIC IDEAL

rosyne—the lovers and givers of splendour, of feasting with dance and song, of enjoyment. In one of his earlier odes Pindar sings their magic power in human life. ' By your aid all things pleasant and sweet are accomplished for mortals, if any man be skilled in song or fair to look upon or hath won renown. Yea, not even the gods order the dance or banquet without the aid of the holy Graces. They are the ministrants of all things in heaven.' In singing their praises Pindar is paying homage to the power of art which flowed in on the consciousness of the Greeks from all the incarnations of beauty in visible or audible form. The Graces enable man to view things for a moment in timeless manner, when his life becomes like that of the gods, free from all thought of disease and decay and death.

And so when the months of physical training have culminated in victory, the arts are called upon to lay their spell also upon the victor and upon all those who are associated with his success. The spiritual delight of music and song and dance enhances still more the idealising interpretation of the poet's words. It is not in general sufficiently remembered that music, which includes for the Greeks song and dance, was, of all the arts, the one which pervaded most intimately their life, the one of which they had the most direct and frequent enjoyment. Painting and sculpture and architecture, though they were all

THE GREEK ATHLETIC IDEAL

in complete harmony with their consciousness, were not so much a part of their lives : such works of art faced them as admirable but independent and objective creations ; in music they all could, and did, indulge in the natural joy of artistic creation, could join together in dance and song in a common unity of self-expression. The actual moment of this activity is felt as something positive and precious during which the cares and desires of life drop away. It is a definite good to be set against the uncertainty of the future and the disappointments of the past. Pindar never tires of insisting upon the wisdom of gathering what the present may offer. Just as the athlete wisely applies his inborn qualities and good training at the right moment and seizes success, so the wise individual will himself employ and share with others the poet's art to appropriate and enjoy to the full a few more moments from the ceaseless progress of time. Victory in the games, numerous as they were, can fall only to a few fortunate individuals ; the enjoyment of art can be seized on countless occasions. This enjoyment comes to men through the inspiration given to poets by the Graces.

Here again the difference between the Greek and the modern conception of athletics appears in its full extent. The intrusion of art into this sphere of life is the seal of seriousness upon what is otherwise idle play, and at the same time makes the seriousness delightful by its own power to charm. We have our photographs and caricatures of athletes and sporting events, and we admire in our own mute manner the harmonious display of skill and physical fairness in some champion, but we do not turn those achievements into a thing of lasting beauty, fresh from generation to generation, full not only with the strength and pride of health, but with a deeper significance drawn from the whole of life. In the days when the leaden breath of Rome hung over Greece and athletics were sunk in the morass of professionalism, St. Paul wondered that men should strive so hard for a corruptible crown. But Pindar always demands something more than the enjoyment of that fragile wreath of olive or wild celery ; his mind is always fixed upon the most incorruptible thing that was possible in his day : ' Whatsoever one hath well said goeth forth with a voice that never dieth ; and thus o'er the fruitful earth and athwart the sea hath passed the light of noble deeds unquenchable for ever.' [1]

And just as he raises the athlete and his success above the temporary limitations of Olympia or Nemea into the wider life of Panhellenic sentiment, so he raises that life to its highest potency. His vision and flight is that of the eagle. ' The eagle swoopeth e'en beyond the sea.' [2] He diffuses into the air by which the common life of

[1] *Isthmians*, 4. 40.   [2] *Nemeans*, 5. 21.

THE GREEK ATHLETIC IDEAL

Greece is sustained a tonic quality which passes with breathing into the blood and stirs the mind to a sudden comprehension of the splendid possibilities of that life. No other Greek poet except the author of the *Odyssey* has transferred into his work so much of the morning freshness of the sea breeze, so much of the brightness of midday, of the clear air through which birds pass, through which ships and islands and steep cliffs and sloping headlands can be seen. As the ship carries him or his song or the victor to Ægina or Sicily or Cyrene, it is met by the gleam of marble temples with their statues and ornaments of gold and bronze. The glory of light is never far from his mind, not only of the day 'child of the sun' in his own beautiful language, but of moonlight shining on a procession of victory or marriage: the brightness of wine and of gold, the brightness of the morning star, of flowers after the dullness of winter; all this light is only the physical or visible counterpart of the light shed on life by the Graces and the poet. The clear bright air and fullness of light felt so directly in these odes stimulates the whole body and mind, acting like wine upon the imagination to raise it to the heroic level. The sap of life seems mounting everywhere, just as the trees and vegetation of the earth grow under the benediction of the morning dew,[1] and the noblest and most incorruptible element in man responds to the precious influence.

[1] *Nemeans*, 8. 40.

THE GREEK ATHLETIC IDEAL

A very slight acquaintance with Pindar's *Odes* will convince the reader that he is free from any narrow admiration of the athlete. The earliest odes are as free from it as the latest; in all of them he comes forward with perfect assurance as the inspired spokesman of Delphic wisdom, confidently bidding his victorious patrons to

> Grow old along with me,
> The best is yet to be,

and he would have the successful athlete advance with him to become the perfect citizen—warrior and counsellor—possessing the things of this world without being possessed by them, turning the bodily and mental training of the early years into a way of life in which the greatest happiness possible for a mortal may be enjoyed. Then only does he become the perfect athlete in the struggle of life. 'For any one man to win the prize of happiness complete is impossible. I cannot say to whom Fate hath proffered this crowning boon as a sure possession. But to thee, Thearion, she giveth a fitting season of success.'[1] As Apollo at Delphi is the exponent of the will of almighty Zeus, so Pindar in his function of poet is the spokesman of Apollo and the wisdom of Delphi. His poetry is full of veneration for the god and his holy place, and through him we have the fullest insight into that gospel of life as it was understood and found acceptable by Greeks from all parts of the

[1] *Nemeans*, 7. 55.

THE GREEK ATHLETIC IDEAL

mainland or Mediterranean, for once united at the festivals of the games.

There is one God, and Apollo is his prophet. That is the beginning and the end of the Delphian or Pindaric theology. Pindar talks much of the other gods, but in his most serious and devout moments he calls upon God without any particular name. He is firmly convinced of his omnipotence and omniscience. 'God fulfilleth every purpose, even as he desireth, God that not only overtaketh the winged eagle, but also surpasseth the dolphin on the sea and bendeth many a proud mortal beneath his sway.'[1] 'If any man hopeth to escape the eye of God, he is grievously wrong.'[2] Trust in God's will is a primary necessity of life, so that the good thing of the present may not be spoiled by anxiety about the future.

And the second great principle of the wisdom of Apollo, more important even than the other for its immediate practical value, is the precept which all visitors to Delphi saw inscribed upon the porch of Apollo's temple : 'Know thyself.' God is unknown, and man, instead of making vain efforts to fathom his mind, had better turn his attention to himself. Know thyself and life as it really is, confined within the limits of the actual, and do not let life pass away in vain hopes which do not recognise what is possible. It is the gospel of mortality, free as yet from the conscious-

[1] *Pythians*, 2. 49.   [2] *Olympians*, 1. 64.

THE GREEK ATHLETIC IDEAL

ness that life is fundamentally insufficient, instinct with the certainty that something can be made of life, not disillusioned, though aware that toil and sorrow come upon all men, and untouched by any belief that in some other world the balance of things may be redressed.

' Learn from me the nature of life '—that is the burden of Pindar's poetry—life which only endures for a limited number of years, exposed through all its course to sickness and sorrow, to toil and weariness with old age as its end, if a man pass unscathed through the dangers of manhood ; a life of effort with hunger and insecurity constantly at the door. Hopes lawful and unlawful, good and bad, dance perpetually before men's eyes, leading by easy stages to delusion and doom. Yet in the years of youth and manhood times and occasions of delight do occur, but without any security of duration, so that the prosperous may fear to fall and the miserable may hope to rise, and the one certainty in life is the uncertainty of fortune.

How salutary for the athlete is Pindar's habitual reference of each success to the wider experience of life ! How necessary where such honour was paid to the victor in the games that he might be tempted in the pride of youth and strength and beauty to think himself to be as one of the glorious gods, who know neither old age nor toil nor disease ! He invests this general knowledge of

THE GREEK ATHLETIC IDEAL

life with all the splendour of language and imagination of which he is capable, and gives it a concrete application in the hour of victory. 'But know thou that for all these things . . .' The warning words come again and again in solemn cadence in almost every ode—it may be to some great Sicilian prince or to the simple athlete from Ægina or Thebes. 'Seek not, my soul, the life of the immortals, but enjoy to the full the resources that are within thy reach.' 'Changeful are the breezes of the winds that blow on high. The bliss of man does not proceed unimpaired for long, whene'er it followeth them in its full weight and measure.'[1] 'If any man who hath riches excelleth others in beauty of form and is wont to display prowess by his courage in the games, let him remember that the limbs he is robing are mortal, and that, in the end of all, he will be clad in a vesture of clay.'[2]

Yet while on the one hand the athlete can see in the clearest manner the limitations of life and the veering currents of human circumstance, on the other hand Pindar bids him rise above helpless insignificance—first, in the faith that whatever happens is the dispensation of Zeus, who gives both 'this and that' and guideth the fate of men that he loveth; secondly, in the knowledge that action, of which this success was but the beginning, is the real life of man and can

[1] *Pythians*, 3. 61 and 104.   [2] *Nemeans*, 11. 13.

THE GREEK ATHLETIC IDEAL

shed upon him something of the glory with which the heroes of the past are invested. The mythical narrative of some hero's prowess, so conspicuous a feature in almost every ode, and possessing for the Greeks the power that the Bible has for Christians, is brought in to reinforce the truths of the preacher. A victory at Olympia or Delphi is not anything final ; it is only the prelude to the more ' swelling theme ' of fine actions accomplished through the whole span of life. And the type of such a life in Pindar's mind is that of Heracles, whose toilsome and beneficent deeds, mingled with those of the Æginetan heroes, Æacus, Peleus, and Achilles, enter so continually with the force of religious influence into the message of these *Odes*. But the heroism of Heracles has its reward. It is not the self-denying heroism of mute service, satisfied with having done its duty. He ' has allotted to him, as his choicest prize, peace that would endure for ever in the homes of bliss,' and man too, bearing in mind the sundering gulf between himself and heaven, may hope to win, with God's grace, delight and happiness from his efforts and to transform the passing delight of success in the games into a more abiding satisfaction, the realisation of the ideal of that wider ' athletic ' life in which we all strive, not for a crown of leaves as in the days of their youth, but for the crowning of their maturity.

' Our limbs are fettered by unfortunate hope,'

THE GREEK ATHLETIC IDEAL

sings Pindar in the last Nemean ode. 'Hope,' he says in a fragment, 'chiefly ruleth the changing heart of man.' In the obscurity of life it is Hope which prompts man to act, and does not let him remain paralysed by his knowledge of the uncertainty of the future. 'We embark upon bold endeavours, yearning after many exploits.'[1] There is the essential character of the Greek, and it is to the training of that character that Pindar addresses himself. Man's hopes and his actions must be concentrated on certain ends which are possible of achievement, and may satisfy his desire for what is fair and noble. 'Youth, by reason of his high hopes, flieth lightly on the wings of his manly exploits.'[2] 'May the gods inspire my love for things fair, while, in the bloom of life, I am eager only for that which is within my power.'[3] 'The brazen heaven he cannot climb.'[4] Vague and romantic desire is to be put away and every purpose and nerve devoted to the accomplishment of something here and now. 'Whatever each man striveth for, if he win it, he must hold it as his near and dear delight.'[5] Such delight may be short-lived or it may be lasting, but it is the highest man can expect, remembering his mortality. 'For every one of all mortal men the brightest boon is the blessing that ever cometh day by day.'[6]

[1] *Nemeans*, 11. 44.   [2] *Pythians*, 8. 90.   [3] *Ibid.*, 11. 51.
[4] *Ibid.*, 10. 27.   [5] *Ibid.*, 10. 61.   [6] *Olympians*, 1. 99.

THE GREEK ATHLETIC IDEAL

And what is the heart's desire? Something that at first sight may seem material enough and yet can expand by the inspiration of Pindar's interpretation to include the delight of art and corporate action. 'Two things alone, linked with the fair flower of wealth, cherish the most delectable bloom of life, even comfort and a fair name.'[1] And more briefly at the end of the first Pythian: 'The first of prizes is comfort; the second is a fair reputation. If a man lights upon and keeps those two things, he has received the highest crown.' That is the ideal of an age when misfortune and want were constantly at the door, and daily bread and bodily security were not always certain. 'Every man strains himself to the task of keeping importunate hunger from his belly.'[2] It is at least a hope that is realisable, and it is not selfish, for a fair reputation can only be won by sharing one's good things with others and thus averting the dangers of envy and falsehood, those two darling sins of the Greek city-state. But comfort and a good name are not enough. Pindar protests against the materialism of his own ideal by insisting on the necessity of winning, where it is possible, a further 'luxurious glory' through art; he dwells on the supreme happiness of those whose actions abide for ever commemorated by the poet's skill. In the midst of this transitory and

[1] *Isthmians*, 5. 12.   [2] *Ibid.*, 1. 49.

uncertain world the poet can establish an unmoved centre of calm where for the moment all else is forgotten in the spell of poetry and the eternity of fame ' promised by the ever-living poet.' ' The light of noble deeds unquenchable for ever.' [1] Such actions attain an ideal or spiritual value as examples for other ages. It is the privilege of princes and of the rich that they most of all can command this immortality, and Pindar, writing primarily for such men, urges them to live up to the measure of this ideal. But he does not lose from sight the mass of men who do not possess distinction of position. They can all share in the ' good work which is done for the common weal.' [2] Every act has its unique value. The individual and his city are ' lit up with countless distinctions by reason of deeds of prowess.' [3] What, after all, are those myths which form the heart of so many odes except narratives of splendid action? Pindar may have been influenced in choosing the myth by the circumstances of the victory which he celebrates, but the full purpose of his choice is not thus narrowly limited. From these myths the consecration of the heroic world falls upon the actual world of men, joining them all together into a ' Church militant.' In that heroic world he finds the ' lust of action ' with which the athlete should be filled in life as well as in the games.

[1] *Isthmians*, 4. 42. [2] *Pythians*, 9. 93. [3] *Nemeans*, 10. 2.

THE GREEK ATHLETIC IDEAL

How intense is the life of those heroes ! Without pause the narrative sweeps along, action following upon action with the swiftness of thought. And, 'though his heart cleaveth fast unto the theme of Heracles,' Pindar sings the noblest form of his ideal in the scene where Pollux 'made no long debate' when he was given the chance of surrendering the fullness of his immortality to redeem from death his mortal brother Castor.[1]

[1] *Nemeans*, 10.

DANCE AND DESIGN IN GREEK LIFE

THE 'eternal form' of the Greeks has long been used as a happy phrase in the criticism of their artistic achievements in sculpture, architecture, and literature, as though all art did not depend upon form. Instead of elucidating the peculiar qualities of the Greek sense of form, criticism has been often too ready to think that the simple application of the word 'form,' as if it possessed in itself some magic power of explanation, was sufficient, making further analysis an impertinence. The more essential matter is to ask in what way did the Greek sense of form first manifest itself, and how was it developed and confirmed in the historical period of which we have knowledge? No doubt a certain propensity to artistic form was natural to the Greek race, yet in its fullest form this power of expression in the plastic arts was not a God-given instinct, but the penetration of one fundamental impulse, aided by long training, through all the activities of life, as occasion for their development gradually occurred. Long before they could build temples or write poems or carve statues they were alive to the spell of form. Where do we find the earliest manifestations of this spirit?

DANCE AND DESIGN IN GREEK LIFE

The Homeric poems are the first comprehensive records of early Greek society that we possess, and it is natural, therefore, to turn to them for information on this subject. What, if any, were the chief artistic activities of the Homeric Greeks ? There is little doubt that the first place must be assigned to music and dancing. Dancing is the earliest, as it is also the most widespread, form of artistic expression among the Greeks, firmly established in all the aspects of life, religious and social, at the very beginning of their history ; and with dancing went music and, sometimes but not always, words. A dance is something lovely or desirable to look upon as well as to take part in ; it satisfies both the creative and contemplative needs of man in his artistic capacity. The Muses dance on Mount Olympus while Apollo makes music for them ; Zeus himself, according to the line of an early Epic poet, preserved by Athenæus,[1] danced in the midst of the other gods. Dancing is associated with the worship of all the greater gods, such as Artemis, Poseidon, Athena, Aphrodite and the Dioscuri. In the first book of the *Iliad*, Apollo is delighted by the dance of the Achæans and lays aside his wrath and stays the plague. Dancing is represented three times on the shield of Achilles—as part of the life of a peaceful city, at the vintaging, and as a separate scene where a dancing place, such as Daidalos

[1] *Athen.*, I. 40.

made in broad Crete for fair-haired Ariadne, is described. Tradition [1] maintained that dancing had always existed in Crete. Odysseus marvelled at the nimble steps of the youths of Phæacia, who were skilled in dancing. It is the boast of Alkinous that his people surpass all men in seafaring, in swiftness of foot, and in dancing and song. Thus there are three aspects of musical dancing in early times : it is used as a religious rite ; it has a social value ; and æsthetically it is delightful for those who take part in it and for those who look on. Experience of it is an integral part of Homeric life. In general considerations of Greek civilisation we pass too easily over this side of their life, because the whole question of Greek music and dancing is obscure, and the lyric or melic poets, with the exception of Pindar's Epinikian odes, have come down to us in a fragmentary state. In his book on Greek lyric poetry Professor Smyth enumerates twenty-one different forms of choral dance and song used for religious and social purposes. All these forms did not exist at the same time, and some of the distinctions may be due to an academic love of classification, though evidence of many other dances too is to be found in Athenæus, whose discussion of dancing and music is a welcome and valuable relief amid

[1] This tradition may conceal the fact that the Homeric Greeks inherited some of their capacity for musical expression with other artistic gifts from the primitive inhabitants of Greece. Cf. *Beloch. Gr. Gesch.*, i. 95.

the indiscriminate trivialities of the *Deipnosophistae*. It is at any rate quite clear that choral music and dance, separately or in combination, were immensely popular; and in the old age of the city-state Plato, looking for a principle of regeneration, wished to make dance and song the principal educational force in the lives of his citizens.

The identity of the predicates 'good' and 'fair' or 'beautiful' in judgments on man's creative activities, which is a cardinal point in Plato's dialogues, occurs in the earliest documents about Greek society. Where we should use the adjective 'good,' the Homeric poet often uses 'fair' or 'beautiful.' 'Though thou art noble,' cries the swineherd Eumæus to the suitor Antinous, 'thou dost not speak fairly or beautifully.' And in the *Iliad* Menelaus says, 'It is not a fair thing to boast to excess.' Of course, the other usage is also established by which fairness is predicated either of human beings or things or those fair works which Athena teaches her favourites without any implication of their ethical or political or social goodness. In the *Iliad* and *Odyssey* beauty is felt by human beings in the contemplation of an action; for instance, listening to a bard reciting legends of glorious deeds, or watching a dance. This is the nearest approach to the use of the word 'beautiful' in modern æsthetics, when an impression received from some external object, quite apart from any practical consideration, is called beautiful. 'This seems to me well-nigh the fairest thing in the world, when a whole people makes merry, and the men sit orderly at feast in the halls, and listen to the singer, and the tables by them are laden with bread and flesh, and a wine bearer drawing the wine serves it round and pours it into the cups.' And in this passage there is the word meaning 'orderly' or 'in order,' which recurs so constantly in the Homeric narrative, and seems to make a connection between the subjective enjoyment of beauty and the practical organisation of life.

This idea of 'orderliness' underlies many of the Homeric judgments about the 'beautiful.' Poseidon says to Apollo, 'Begin, for thou art younger; it were not fair for me, since I was born first and know more.' The orderliness of the family organisation is something fair in itself, and must not be broken into. When Telemachus and his friend visit Nestor in quest of Odysseus, Nestor says, 'Now is a fairer time to inquire and ask the strangers who they are, now that they have had their delight of food.' Here it is the rites of hospitality, the duty of host to guest, which constitutes something fair, which it is pleasant to contemplate. So, too, Ctesippus, one of the suitors of Penelope, says, 'Hear me, ye lordly wooers . . . the stranger has long had his due portion, as is meet, an equal share ; for it is not fair nor just to rob the guests of their right, whosoever they may be that come to this house.' This passage is the more interesting because 'fair' is joined with 'just,' an adjective that is only used in moral judgment. And in Priam's famous utterance about the death of the young on the field of battle there is a recognition of death itself as something that has 'fairness,' when it falls in with established order. 'A young man all beseemeth even to be slain in war, to be torn by the sharp bronze and lie on the field, though he be dead, yet it is fair for him, whate'er be seen.'[1] That the young should fight is part of the established order of society, and no hideousness of details can mar the form of that action.

Pallas Athene is the inspirer of warlike spirit as well as of handicraft. She gave the Phœnicians notable wisdom in all fair handiwork. She is the giver of form. 'The first sign of Athena's presence with any people,' says Ruskin, 'is that they become warriors, and that the chief thought of every man of them is to stand rightly in his rank, and not fail from his brother's side in battle.' And in *The Queen of the Air* he has described with eloquence and imagination how she is the inspirer for women to weave aright the colours into patterns on the loom; the patron goddess of orderliness in battle and in domestic work, of music; as

[1] Homer, *Odyssey*, trans. Butcher and Lang; *Iliad*, Leaf Lang, Myers. (Macmillans.)

goddess of the clear sky, she is for men the power of clearness and prudence in counsel, and in this way we find her associated with Odysseus. The principle, the distinguishing mark of all these arts, is the orderliness of the work shown in design on robes such as that used in the great Panathenaic procession, the rhythm of music, the clearness of form in vases or sculpture or temple. The effect of Athena's work on the beholder is described by the word 'graceful' ($\chi\alpha\rho\acute{\iota}\epsilon\nu$), or ' that which causes delight,' and this effect is aroused by the clearness and order of the form—what we call design.

Thus in Homer beauty or fairness is attributed to things by virtue of a quality of orderliness. The excellence of a bard's recitation is that he sings in orderly fashion of the faring of the Achæans. The same word ($\kappa\acute{o}\sigma\mu o\varsigma$) is used of the orderly arrangement of troops and of strictly artistic works, such as ornaments for women or horses, and Plato employs it to describe the universe created and guided by the spirit of God. And this quality, in which the Homeric writer finds the beauty of human activity no less than of things created by man, may reasonably be expected to be present in his own poetical form. Walter Pater has quite casually put forward the problem of beauty in the Homeric poems in a well-known chapter of *Marius the Epicurean*:

" οἱ δ'ὅτε δὴ λιμένος πολυβενθέος ἐντὸς ἵκοντο
ἵστια μὲν στείλαντο, θέσαν δ'ἐν νηὶ μελαίνῃ

DANCE AND DESIGN IN GREEK LIFE

ἴστον δ'ἱστοδόκῃ πέλασαν προτόνοισιν ὑφέντες
καρπαλίμως, τὴν δ'εἰς ὅρμον προέρεσσαν ἐρετμοῖς.

When they were now entered within the deep haven, they furled their sails and laid them in the black ship, and lowered the mast by the forestays and brought it to the crutch with speed, and rowed her with oars to the anchorage.

How poetic the simple incident seemed, told just thus ! . . . And one might think there had been no effort in it ; that here was but the almost mechanical transcript of a time, naturally, instinctively poetic, a time in which one could hardly have spoken at all without ideal effect, or the sailors pulled down their boat without making a picture in the ' great style ' against a sky charged with marvels. Or might the closer student discover even here, even in Homer, the really mediatorial function of the poet . . . the poet waiting, so to speak, in an age which had felt itself trite and commonplace enough, on this opportunity for the touch of ' golden alchemy ' ? " Surely the ' golden alchemy ' of this passage and of the mass of Homeric narrative is the exquisite orderliness or clearness of design, the sudden limiting of our vision to certain facts and forms, with an intensifying effect similar to that experienced when the blue sky suddenly receives form, seen through a railway arch or between the pillars of a ruined temple. The peculiar nature of beauty for the Greeks and our power to appreciate it can

DANCE AND DESIGN IN GREEK LIFE

be tested by our enjoyment, not of particular books or passages in Homer, but of the general narrative, with its continual repetition of lines and phrases and epithets, the form of each separate lay or incident sung by the rhapsodist.

Now this spirit of orderliness or form is conspicuously present in Greek dancing until the second half of the fifth century. As an activity which men delight to take part in, or as a spectacle which they can contemplate with pleasure, it is something fair or beautiful. The religious significance of the dance stamps it as something good as well as fair. As part of the service of the gods united with music and words, it became a hymn expressing religious sentiment. It was also connected with two most important occasions, marriage and death; both these forms of dance occur in Homer, and they were subsequently developed into the dirge and epithalamium, while the other various emotions of life found expression in dithyramb, epinikion, hyporcheme, scolion. From this association of the movements of the choral dance as something used in the service of the gods, and pleasing to them, it is but a short step to the identification of what is good and beautiful. Beautiful the dance was both for men and gods, for the gods themselves enjoyed dancing; and if the gods loved what was good and just, then the dance too, which had the power to turn away their wrath against men, must be something good

DANCE AND DESIGN IN GREEK LIFE

in itself. Thus, while the word 'beautiful' or 'fair' might be predicated of an object such as the moon or the dew by Sappho, without any suggestion of goodness about it, there was always present to the Greek the wider and deeper significance of the word in which goodness, implying the satisfaction and approval of heaven, was included. In this manner goodness became associated with order and design by the employment and regulation of a common activity to express religious service as well as the other emotional needs of life.

If we reduce Greek dancing to its simplest form, we find that it is rhythmical movement hardly different from walking, except that each step, as well as the whole dance, has a definite spatial and temporal period assigned to it, and that the time is given by music of a simple sort. The distinguishing qualities of it are precision and orderliness of movement performed by the whole body. The union of song, music and dance was looked on as the highest form of art in this kind of production, and it is beautiful by reason of the harmonious pattern which man could design for himself out of those materials, just as he could organise himself fairly for battle, for the entertainment of a friend, and in the ordered course of a feast. Nor must it be forgotten that the movement of the arms was no less important than that of the legs, and that the

DANCE AND DESIGN IN GREEK LIFE

gestures of the body expressed dumbly the sentiment of the words to which also the form of music corresponded. Thus the form of the dance entered into the individual through three separate channels, and as an educative influence far surpassed any training that subsequent ages have devised. And it was not only the young, whether boys or girls, who danced even in pre-Homeric times. All men of military age danced, as in the Pæan to Apollo, and the advance to battle is little less than a form of dance. The contrast between the Achæans and the barbarians in the *Iliad* is shown by the silent orderliness or harmony of the Achæan advance, while the Trojans come on with disordered cries out of relation to the measured step of military order. The love of dancing—and with that love, of necessity, went a feeling for the form of it—was ingrained in the Greeks long before it became an essential part of primary and secondary education. It was the medium in which they first developed their sense of form, in which they were all artists, for at one time or another they all learned to express their emotions and to create artistic form in the dance. Thus artistic form came to them to be not something exceptional, demanding a peculiar effort or attitude for comprehension, but a form in which they naturally arranged things.

Much of our knowledge of Greek dancing comes from scenes on vases and reliefs. We know

DANCE AND DESIGN IN GREEK LIFE

that during the centuries of development the music was kept strictly subordinate to the dance and the words ; that dancing included processional marches as well as formal figures ; that rhythm of words and movement was inextricably woven together, the same words being used indifferently in both spheres to accompany the movement of metre or step. From the vases we learn much about the attitudes of arms and legs and of the body as a whole. Angularity of gesture seems very predominant and carries with it strong opposition of line between the various limbs. Down to the middle of the fifth century tumultuous and highly complicated forms of musical dance were not favoured, and in the absence of professional dancers the actual movements must have lacked the precision and multiplicity of the modern ballet dancing. Maurice Emmanuel has drawn attention to these facts in his book on the Greek dance. But in all cases the demand for clearness and sharpness of form is apparent, as in the simple stanzas of the Æolian lyric poets, while the responsions in Pindar's more elaborate odes show that the general susceptibility of the Greek to delicate resemblances and differences was highly developed. And while on certain occasions individuals may have danced alone, the mass of this dancing, like the mass of choral lyric, was presented as part of the life of society. Even Sappho's poems, personal though they

DANCE AND DESIGN IN GREEK LIFE

may seem, were written for the occasions of her circle.

Let us attempt to sum up more precisely the peculiar qualities of the dance which made it not only æsthetically delightful, but morally valuable to the Greeks, so that in historical times they gave it the principal place in their educational system. And this educational employment of dance and music did not lessen, as might be expected, their attraction as modes of pleasure for the Greek long after he had passed into manhood ; the moral as well as the æsthetic influence remained with him, encouraging and demanding always unity of design and decorative value in all the forms of self-expression. The relationship of parts to whole was all-important, and the whole was enjoyed, not as having any meaning or suggestion beyond itself, but as a piece of decoration, delighting by the clearness and harmonious completeness of its form. They felt a deep enjoyment in performing or seeing a certain pattern of rhythmical movement in which there was still room for slight personal variations without spoiling the general regularity, so that the individual moved with the freedom of self-imposed law in the general scheme. There was no excessive obtrusion of this or that individual—he was essentially a member of a chorus ; nor was the 'virtuosity' of one member, though it might make to superficial eyes the beauty of the whole, important any more than the beauty of a Doric temple depended upon some particular decoration added to the essential form. The beauty resided in the rational order of the whole, obvious to all, and in proportion as the Greeks failed to find this rational order in the external world which was not of their creating, so they rejoiced to achieve it in works of art, where the matter could be more satisfactorily moulded to their heart's desire. And music and dance are among artistic creations those that are least subject to the disorganising accidents of alien material.

It is, then, through this ideal of rational orderliness that the division between æsthetic and social or ethical values disappears for the Greeks, and we are never troubled during the period of their growth and greatness by any suggestion of that opposition between life and art which has vexed subsequent ages. A remark in Athenæus,[1] made during a discussion of dancing, illustrates most completely the identity of ethical and æsthetic judgments : 'In dancing and walking gracefulness and order are beautiful, disorder and vulgarity are ugly.' The words translated by order and disorder ($\kappa\acute{o}\sigma\mu o\varsigma, \dot{a}\tau a\xi\acute{\iota}a$) are continually employed in ethical writings; and it is characteristic, too, of the Greek outlook to exact their artistic or æsthetic standard in the lesser

[1] *Athen.*, xiv. 25.

DANCE AND DESIGN IN GREEK LIFE

matters of life, such as walking and dressing; attention to such matters brings 'orderliness and pleasure' into life.[1] It is their aim to realise everywhere in the social organisations of life the ideal which their æsthetic sense approved and education had confirmed, and that ideal is a rational harmony of design. It was their inability to discover such a design in the totality of experience that caused them such perplexity about the government of the gods, and an openly confessed fear and even rejection of life. But when they are describing human institutions their tone is very different. Listen to Solon's description of the effects of good laws in a city. His phraseology would be no less suitable in describing the appearance of a well-ordered dance: 'Good laws bring order and evenness into a state; they smooth what is rough, stop excess, make arrogance to disappear, straighten out what is crooked, check disagreement.' The image lying behind this ideal state of society is that of a balanced pattern or design—a 'mazy dance'— in which there is no room for the individual to be obtrusive or arrogant; the design is carried out evenly without check or irregularity. The Greek feeling in social matters was against the prominence of one member over the rest,[2] just as in their art one part was never emphasised at the expense of the rest. In their sculpture or architecture they

[1] *Ibid.*, i. 38.   [2] Cf. *Ostracism at Athens*.

DANCE AND DESIGN IN GREEK LIFE

never concentrated on effects of beauty in the face or the column until the period of decadence ; their beauty was something spread over the whole body or building, and the face or column shared in it proportionately. Preoccupation with facial expression, such as we find in Leonardo's painting, would be repellent to their artistic sense.

This desire to find and enjoy rational order is, as we have said, at the basis of the Greek fear of life. It can be traced everywhere in their literature before the Periclean age. It appears most conspicuously in Theognis and Herodotus. ' Danger hangs over all action,' says the former, ' nor does any man know at the beginning of an action how it will end. He who expects to win glory unexpectedly falls into great and grievous trouble.' Helplessness ($ἀμηχανίη$) encompasses human beings on all sides, and man's best prayer is to ask the gods for a release or solution ($ἔκλυσις$) from the difficulties of life. The use of such language is an admission of failure to find a fixed plan in the dealings of heaven, and after Æschylus, who wrestled all his life with this problem, we find no writer attempting to justify the ways of God to man. Sophocles, who was in the opinion of his own age a religious nature, preaches a pious resignation to God's will as inscrutable and inevitable. Yet in all these writers the fundamental æsthetic judgment of the Greeks asserts itself in the belief that Zeus brings low the man who exceeds a certain measure and raises his head too high. Arrogance or high position, though achieved without sin, draw upon themselves the visitation of the divine power, because they make irregular what should be regular. Such irregularities are transgressions, a stepping out of the design (ὑπερβασία). 'Thy power, O Zeus,' sings the chorus in the *Antigone*, 'what transgression of man can set at nought?' Here the poet suggests that, unknown to man, there is a mysterious plan according to which our actions are regulated; but most Greeks would not accept such unreasoning quietism. Again, it was undoubtedly from the same æsthetic influence that they would not pass verdict upon an individual life before the end had come. Herodotus has given the most memorable expression to this feeling in the episode of Crœsus and Solon; it implies that the happiness of an individual life depends upon the completion of a certain pattern in it. What that pattern was in Herodotus's opinion is clear from the stories of Tellos and Cleobis and Biton with which Solon humbled the pride of the incredulous Crœsus.

The word 'dike,' which, in the classical period, is the ordinary equivalent for 'justice,' also has the meaning of 'manner' or 'way.' This usage is established in Homer to describe the practice of men moving along a prescribed or customary way, and we can see how the Greek words for our 'sin' (ἁμαρτία, ὑπερβασία) carry on the same mode of thought. In philosophic writers the word acquired an almost technical significance, yet the well-known passage in the *Laws*, though it may contain Pythagorean influences, has much which is only the natural development of ordinary Greek conceptions. There it is said that God, who possesses in himself the beginning and middle and end of all things—the great Designer—journeys along an undeviating path, followed by Justice, to whom cling all of humble and orderly disposition who wish for happiness. This passage, with its figurative idea of God's progress, recalls the *Myth of the Phædrus*, when the Beatific Vision is witnessed by the souls in the spectacle of a divine procession or dance, in which we are told that envy has no place. The god of Plato is very far from the primitive gods of the first Greek settlers, but the difference is a quantitative one of spiritual content. Plato has heightened the spiritual significance of the early gods, personifications, for the most part, of natural phenomena, of the powers of light moving in the heavens. From the movements of these bodies the Greeks, long before they had settled into their final habitations in Greece, drew their first observations of regularity, which, uniting with their peculiar natural endowment, formed in the end their wonderful artistic genius. Yet the regularity of the heavenly bodies was not always perfect—variations occurred of which they could find no

DANCE AND DESIGN IN GREEK LIFE

explanation; but the charm of that spectacle remained always—the heavenly type of dance; and in one of his most poetic odes Sophocles addressed the god Dionysus as 'leader of the dance of the fiery stars.'

We can observe the same idea in the function of the individual in the city-state: a tendency to realise artistic form constantly prevails. Within the limits of their own states the Greeks were certainly organised, but it was self-organisation—they gave themselves form, they did not receive it from outside; and geographical conditions, as well as the constitution of their own minds, never allowed the sense of form to be lost; the individual could grasp the design of the whole. In their early wanderings the Greeks possessed a certain social form: there were clans, based on the unit of the family, descended from a common ancestor; the phratry was an intermediate unit 'of religious significance.' In the constitution of Cleisthenes and in the period after the Persian wars the final harmony of social and political form was achieved. This organisation gave full expression to their nature in a state that was an end in itself, and it was only in the second half of the fifth century B.C., when great power was practically forced on the Athenians, that the necessities of imperial government broke the harmony. The inherent falseness of the Periclean organisation is shown by the speedy collapse of Athens as soon as his genius had ceased to impose itself on the mass of the citizens. During his rule the mind of the public became perverted. The imperialistic gospel of the modern world—the will to expand—has exalted too much the achievement of Athenian domination, and we are called on to admire above all else these energetic empire builders and to find in the Periclean age the most precious heritage of Greece. Yet the great writers who lived in it and after it—Thucydides, Aristophanes, Euripides—all recognise the failure of the past decades, Thucydides most of all by silently contrasting the ideals of the Periclean Oration with the realities of Athenian policy when it was called upon to direct itself.

The great distinction of the spiritual law of the Greeks is that it was not revealed to them by a divine lawgiver, nor was it adopted from other nations in the way in which we have taken much of our religious and other spiritual values from the East and from the Greeks and Romans. The phraseology in which they expressed their thought is no longer peculiar to them; through their literature it has become the unconscious possession of modern civilisation. But their unique chance, wherein they have the advantage over all who have followed them in time, was to have been able to lay their own foundations,[1] and to develop upon

[1] What they received from others was completely absorbed and remoulded by their genius and became practically their own creation.

DANCE AND DESIGN IN GREEK LIFE

them their own culture; and so a perfectly organic structure arose, pervaded everywhere by the one plastic force. Here, for once, man achieved a complete fusion of practical and æsthetic modes of thought ; the standard applied to the different activities of life was always the same. It is this which constitutes for the modern world the attraction and the pathos of the Greek genius. Our life is broken into countless unharmonised varieties of experience ; we strain after the unity which was their natural possession. Our position as their heirs and as the heirs of many other peoples condemns our longing to be for ever unsatisfied, and the longing itself is worth little. The duty of the living is to create, not to receive form from the past. And, originally, how fragile was the form in which the life of Greece and Athens was housed ! The Confederacy of Delos was the beginning of the end, and with the transference of the executive power to Athens organised empire was born into the world. Efficiency took the place of spontaneous self-development.

> A brittle glory shineth in this face :
> As brittle as the glory is the face.

AN ASPECT OF EDUCATION IN PLATO'S 'LAWS'

THERE is a curious passage in the seventh book [1] of the *Laws* in which the Athenian, who is the mouthpiece of Plato throughout the work, discusses the relationship of 'play' or 'amusement' and 'earnestness' (παιδιά, σπουδή) in the society of that time. God alone, he says, is a matter for the greatest earnestness; human affairs deserve but little. Man is the plaything of God, and at his best can only give pleasure to God; he should therefore pass his life in the performance of the fairest amusements, sacrifice, dance, and song. In the same spirit he goes on to protest against the arbitrary division of human life into things earnest and amusing; the whole of life should rather be the expression of one spirit, not an alternation of purposes. And asking what the most earnest thing for mankind is, he replies, jesting on the verbal resemblance of the two words (παιδιά, παιδεία), play and education. Humanity should go through life amusing itself by the game of education; he does not mean technical education; the combination with παιδιά raises it into a pleasurable and artistic form in which men can take delight. This education is the most 'earnest'

[1] 803 B *seq.*

AN ASPECT OF EDUCATION

thing which man can do, and by it he grows most welcome to God, and therefore God-like. Viewed from the human standpoint, it may be called amusement ; viewed according to the will of God, it is the most earnest of all things. The Spartan, catching only the literal meaning of the Athenian's remark that human affairs deserve little earnestness, is shocked by his pessimistic view of the world, and the discussion reverts abruptly to a consideration of practical details. Yet this treatment of 'earnestness' and 'play' is of capital importance for the understanding of Plato's educational point of view in the *Laws*; in almost every book there is a reference either in jest or seriousness to this conception of human affairs. It is an emphatic protest against the division of human powers, and an assertion that every part of man's activities must be directed and absorbed by a single purpose. The whole of society is to work together to realise its own peculiar excellence (ἀρετή), and the process by which it is to be realised is education.

This idea of unity attaining consciousness and perfection in the organisation of all individual wills has been transferred by Plato from the artistic to the moral and social world. The State as imagined in the *Laws*, far more than in the *Republic*, is to be in all truth a work of art, not created in colour or marble or words, but in the harmonious structure of living wills. This conception of the State was always in Plato's mind, and may have been the cause of his harsh treatment of artists, so far as they claimed to create freed from all the restrictions of the society in which they lived. He knew well the power that art can exercise upon men, and did not wish that such an influence should be allowed to exist unsubdued to the purpose of the whole. Such particular activities as the enjoyment of a tragedy or poem or musical dance must be subordinated to the wider enjoyment of the State as a work of art, and citizens must be taught to look for supreme artistic enjoyment nowhere else but in the creation and maintenance of that greatest of all works of art, in which the creative and contemplative faculty of enjoyment in every man and not a limited number can be satisfied. Logically considered, the Platonic treatment of artists is not one-sided or severe. It will be only in the first stages of the new State that repressive or exclusive measures have to be taken. Then especially it is necessary that all the influences within the State should tend in one direction. Once this system of education is started and steadily pursuing its course, the citizens of creative artistic power will naturally produce that kind of art which Plato wishes to encourage. For the artists themselves will have passed through the same education as the other citizens. The ideals of life and State will have entered into their being through dance

AN ASPECT OF EDUCATION

and song, and, when the creative instinct awakes in them, they will tend, like the artists of the fifth century B.C. or in the Pre-Raphaelite age, to give plastic form to what they recognise as the supreme reality. The true artist does not toil for years to create what is formless or without value to men; his art is an opportunity for him to show the reality that lies in experience. In the fourteenth century that reality was the Gospel story; in Plato's mind it is the reality of the State. In the expression of those experiences, where lesser men have equal freedom to produce with greater, there is bound to be stiffness and monotony of representation, but there will be no weakness of sentiment or suffering in the expression, if their wills are striving to realise something greater and diviner than themselves.

In the seventh book [1] Plato expresses this larger view of art in reply to a band of tragic poets, desirous of giving performances in the new State: 'My friends, we are, so far as in us lies, the composers of the best and fairest tragedy of all; for this whole State of ours is an imitation of the best and fairest life, and that in our opinion is the truest tragedy. So then we are rivals with you in the production of the most beautiful drama which true laws only can produce. You must not, therefore, expect us to allow you free entrance and permission to play what you will. . . .' It is one

[1] 817 B *seq.*

IN PLATO'S 'LAWS'

of the passages where the genius of Plato burns up in the midst of the prescriptions and advice to the founders of the Cretan colony. He views this common life of men in a State as an immense drama, the most serious that can be played, the imitation in reality of the fairest form of life that man can imagine. But in this drama of our common life the hero is a noble humanity, not one great man; the organism of society takes the place of the individual, not only able to have the idea of this drama stored in consciousness, but to enjoy the task of realising it. Each citizen was to have developed in himself the pride of being a performer in this drama, and also the true artistic pleasure of being able to contemplate the great work as a completed spectacle.

How powerful Plato felt the influence of art in a State may become, is shown by a passage towards the end of the third book,[1] where he traces the beginning of Athenian political degeneration to the failure of taste in artistic matters. A gradual lawlessness about poetic style grew up among musicians ignorant of the justice and law of the Muses and overcome by the passion of pleasure. The caprice of the individual was held to be the only standard, and every one was encouraged to regard his own feelings as a sound judge. From the theatre this licence naturally spread to the ecclesia, and infected the whole life of the State with the diseased

[1] 700 A *seq.*

belief that any one was entitled to expect consideration of his opinion, and need feel no respect for the views of those who were morally and intellectually better men. No better proof could be found of the 'earnestness' which Plato thought was the true essence of 'play' or 'amusement.' In the same spirit, when discussing the games of children, he deprecates any alteration of the established forms as calculated to induce an unstable and changeable habit of mind and body. Plato does not consider either games or theatrical performances the most important things in a State; the importance they possess is due to the fact that they are two spheres of life, where taste is first formed and freely displayed by the ordinary mind, which feels that such matters, having little or no connection with political or religious duties, are in themselves unimportant. It is one of the many places in the *Laws* where Plato makes use of history to prove that it is impossible to neglect any department, however trivial it may seem, of man's life without running the risk of weakness spreading from it to more dangerous localities.

Plato desired the habit of æsthetic enjoyment to be developed as part of the general education of the young. The appreciation of art was not to be left as an uncharted country into which some might penetrate in later years, while others might remain oblivious of it or develop a perverse or exaggerated taste. The education of the young, he says in the second book [1] of the *Laws*, is little more than the correct management of pleasure and affection and pain and dislike in their souls, first of all in unreasoning fashion and then with reasonable conviction, so that the regulation of those emotions may coincide with the rational principle in man. These emotions of pleasure and pain, etc., are liable to degeneration in the process of life, were it not that heaven has given us a natural love of orderly movement, a pleasurable perception of rhythm in dance and song with the desire to imitate such things for ourselves; this natural enjoyment is strong in children, and we can therefore rightly describe the earliest form of education as the gift of Apollo and the Muses, and in those first stages achieve the unity, both of artistic pleasure in the re-creation of a work of art in dance or song and of morality expressing itself in those words and rhythms. For there are two points to bear carefully in mind when considering Plato's views about the educational use of choric dancing and singing in the early books of the *Laws*. The Greeks must have been far more susceptible than we are to the artistic effect of choric music. We are not in general profoundly moved by it; we have ample evidence that the Greeks were delighted by what would seem to us to be the most austere music and dance. Secondly, ideas, which we have to express in words, they

[1] 653 A, B.

AN ASPECT OF EDUCATION

were able to express and interpret with equal facility by gesture in dance and musical rhythm and tone. The simplest forms of music and dance exercised upon them an influence not unlike that which Wordsworth describes as being exercised by Nature on her favoured children, something that becomes 'interfused' with their very being:

> The floating clouds their state shall lend
> To her: for her the willow bend;
>   Nor shall she fail to see
> Even in the motion of the storm
> Grace that shall mould the maiden form
>   By silent sympathy.
> .   .   .   .   .
> And beauty born of murmuring sound
>   Shall pass into her face.

So in a similar manner Plato holds that moral qualities by the form of rhythmical movement into which they are translated, instead of confronting the spectator as nothing better than a lesson, pass by his own action into the body and so into the soul, and ceasing to be a matter of imitation become in time a real element of his nature.

Of these choric bands or choruses there are to be three kinds in the State: one composed of the young, another of those up to the age of thirty, a third of those between thirty and sixty years.[1] The whole population, male and female, freeman and slave, is to be enrolled in these choric dances

[1] 664-5.

The form and content of the dance, *i.e.* the words, music, and gesture, can admit little variation in the general nature of their subject-matter, though variety in the detail of expression is for obvious reasons to be encouraged. The theme is to be the identity of pleasure and goodness, of justice and beauty : the happiness and pleasure of the good life : the unhappiness of the unjust life, though it be accompanied by all beauty and wealth and health : the approval of heaven upon the good life as being also the most pleasant. This insistence on a right sense of pleasure is due to the importance to the young of correct ideas on that subject. The elders over sixty, who may also form a chorus under the inspiration of Dionysus, are to act as a board to exercise supervision over the whole body of State music, to whom new productions may be shown, and who by example and precept may help on the development of the younger generations. Plato comes back again and again to the assertion that education is primarily the leading or directing of the young to the service of true reason, and it is the elders who know most about law and reason. They have the fuller knowledge necessary to judge music, not merely by the standard of pleasure but by its goodness. Pleasure by itself is the feeblest of all standards,[1] for it is aroused merely by correct imitation of something. There

[1] 667.

must be a fuller content for the arts that are part of the life of a State, something that is more than a harmless pleasure, and brings benefit with it by making the moral law welcome to the wills that take part in those rites. For the performances of these choric dances would not be very dissimilar from the ritual ceremonies of a church performed with solemn and punctilious observance. There is in each case a consecrated form of liturgy, words and music and movement woven together, though in the church service the priest represents the whole congregation, who are content to follow in spirit, while in the ancient chorus there was community of action as well as thought. In both cases there is no need or desire of novelty, for the service is in honour of an unchanging God, while in the choric performance the danger of indifference that lurks in repetition is lessened by the active participation of each member. The religious service and choric dance are both alike in that they exercise a spell upon the performer and spectator. In several places Plato uses the word 'spell' to describe the effect of these art-forms upon the young, and we often use the word in describing the effect of great works of art. We know, what Plato with his shorter historical perspective could only divine, that the greatness and power of art does not depend on novelty or strangeness of subject-matter. The Delphic charioteer, the figures from Ægina or the Par-

IN PLATO'S 'LAWS'

thenon, the simple forms of Francesca's and Giovanni Bellini's pictures repeated over and over again, possess a solemn hieratic quality which is the visual counterpart of the simplicity and majesty of the moral law. They show how much can be achieved with a limited subject-matter if only the artist is great enough to re-create and not to adapt the types he has received. Greek art of the fifth century was indifferent to originality of subject or treatment in the superficial sense, and Plato's restrictions upon artists seem illiberal or intolerant to an age like the fourth century B.C. that lacks deep genius, and can only refine upon or exaggerate existing forms. It is the law and self-limitation that gives the real and higher freedom in these matters.

In justice to Plato it must be remembered that his censorship of artists is exercised in the interest of what he thought more important than art, namely, the State as a social, political, and religious unity. In the fourth century B.C., as in the late fifteenth and sixteenth centuries A.D., artists broke away from the service of religion as the supreme reality in life, and claimed to realise an end of their own, to give expression to a reality independent of other spiritual ideals. Plato would call that movement a degeneration of art from 'earnestness' to 'amusement,' and a renunciation of the higher values of art. Much of the difficulty in understanding his criticism of music

AN ASPECT OF EDUCATION

in this part of the *Laws* is due to these two standpoints from which he judges the creations of art ; where they are viewed as amusements, where correctness of form only is desired, pleasure is the standard by which they are judged ; if as something earnest, then some kind of moral benefit and purpose must be their justification. Further, when choric music is rightly employed, the delight that the participants experience in it is a feeling of physical good health or vitality. The body performs that which is in harmony with its true nature, giving physical expression to the law of its being, and thereby the highest pleasure not only to itself but to those who, owing to their age, instead of taking part in, are forced to contemplate, those art-forms. In either case the individual receives a vital or tonic impulse in his life.

Nor would Plato separate this feeling from that which comes after the performance of any action that is in harmony with the law of the State. His view of life is surely the wider and deeper, postulating a unity and protesting against the diffusion of interests and the breaking up of reality into independent spiritual activities. With us artistic, social, political, religious ideals are in continual conflict, or else ignore each other. We cannot bring ourselves to be collectively in earnest about any of them. But Plato seems in the *Laws* to be even more in earnest about the practical possibility of his theory than in the *Republic*, and, in accordance with this purpose, considers the needs of the ordinary man who forms the mass of citizens. It is the chief glory of the *Laws* that they are a solitary attempt to sketch a fundamental system of education for a whole State, dealing most comprehensively with the possibilities of the whole people and not the intellectually advanced. Time had probably taught Plato that a regeneration of society could not be effected by an auspiciously endowed tyrant or class of philosopher-guardians unless they began their reforming work at the basis of society ; anything else would turn out to be only a partial or superficial alteration. The provisions of the *Laws* are dictated by a consideration of what the ordinary mass of citizens require. In what way can the higher interests and spiritual activities of man be used, not as simple amusements or intellectual delights for him, but as means to influence the whole life of the society in which he exists ? How can amusements, while still possessing the attraction of amusements, accomplish something ' earnest ' as well ? In his own experience of life Plato must have been struck by the disparity between the few, who understood and enjoy art, and the masses who found, at all events in dramatic and choric performances, simply an occasion of idle amusement. Great powers of mind and influence were being lost or disregarded, either from a solitary cultivation of

AN ASPECT OF EDUCATION

art for art's sake, or from a desire to be popular by amusing the crowd. The power of poetry, music, singing, and dancing over the Greek people was indisputable : the problem for Plato was how this faculty of enjoyment might be almost unconsciously utilised for the purpose of educating society.

It is the formation of standards of taste in the masses that is wanted far more than technical proficiency in reading or writing or counting ; these parts of education are treated in very cursory fashion by Plato, who saw that real progress does not rest on efficiency of that kind, but on the quality of life that is desired and lived by the citizens. Nor does he intend taste to be an absolute power of criticism, based on a knowledge of rules for certain arts, and exercised only on some material that is not a part of the corporate life, as, for instance, in the modern world a picture gallery or a concert hall is looked on as the rightful place for the exercise of taste. He wishes taste to be formed organically by the individual experiencing instead of simply seeing what is good or beautiful. In this respect Plato has an immense superiority over the modern educator for whom choric music and dance has fallen into neglect as an educational subject.[1] The value of personal co-operation is lost in those arts which rest on the

[1] There are signs of revival at the present day, for instance, in the Dalcroze school of dancing.

IN PLATO'S 'LAWS'

opposition of subject and object. Fully educated taste was in Plato's view a way of life self-imposed by each citizen. It was not to be kept narrow by exercise only in artistic amusement; amusement itself was to be deepened and given that very necessary 'earnest' quality by being brought into direct relation with the social, political, and religious life of the State. On all art-forms there is to rest religious approbation. In the *Laws* there is little distinction between religious and political justification; God, we are told, is the beginning, the end, the middle, and the measure of all things.[1] Man's duty to him is to ask what kind of action is pleasing to him, and so to live. All men must believe in his reality and follow out his will as expressed in the law of the State. He is the final consecration and sanction upon all institutions, and obedience to those institutions and reverence in the service of heaven and devotion to the memory of dead heroes and ancestors is the true religious life of the citizen. So, when Plato aims at making art serviceable to political life, he is really trying to establish a tradition of religious art which will be immune from change by the scrupulous respect which it inspires.

In the choric dance, words, music, and motions repeat with threefold emphasis the content of moral precept. The Greeks excelled in dignified expression of general moral truths, and in

[1] 716.

AN ASPECT OF EDUCATION

criticising Plato's desire to keep artists to the expression of moral precept we must remember simple truths can receive abiding and impressive form from the artist's personality. The tragedians were

> teachers best
> Of moral prudence with delight received
> In brief sententious precept.

And much of the greatest art in the world exercises a religious or moral effect by investing the simple forms of life with a sudden significance. Further, the reception of these moral precepts in artistic activity was not to be confined within a short period of years; they were to be kept a fresh and active principle of action in men by continuous participation until the arrival of old age. If the earlier training has been successful, the perfected formation of taste or complete education is shown by each individual regarding of his own accord the whole extent of his life as a field in which to realise his enlarged consciousness of goodness and pleasure. Choric dance and musical festival are no longer relaxations from the business of life, but variations in the form of the one political activity carried on everywhere in the same spirit. The life of the whole State becomes in the truest and finest sense a work of art.

The simplicity or limitation of art's function in this State need not lower the dignity or beauty of that service. Any attempt to alter or raise taste must begin in the simplest form. Expositions of rare or difficult artistic work can have no effect on an uncultured audience; the pearls are not recognised as desirable or even possible food. And the artist, too, whom Plato is thought to deal so harshly with, need not disdain his task. Instead of pursuing a lonely self-satisfaction or the approval of a few 'finer souls,' he is required to take his part in that much wider work which is the building of the City of God. There is the vision of supreme reality to stir his emotions and fire his hand. Inspiration cannot be forced; yet Italian painting of the fourteenth and fifteenth centuries shows that limitation of subject does not cramp an artist or weaken his power of appeal, provided that the public and he are both convinced of the truth of the ideal that they are trying to realise. That 'synoptic' vision which Plato defined in the *Republic* as the mark of the true philosopher remained with him in the educational theory of the *Laws*, transmuting the prescriptions for a small city-state into principles of abiding value for humanity. In summing up Plato's conception in the *Laws* of the function of art, with particular regard to song and dance, in the State, we may say that he desired the artistic tastes and creative impulses of men to be used for political purposes, and not to be treated as mere pastimes or amusements (παιδιαί), out of relation to the practical side of experience. Protesting against the conventional division of life into

AN ASPECT OF EDUCATION

things serious or amusing, and the consequent limitation of art to the sphere of amusements, he attempts to remove the antithesis by combining the two apparent opposites in the wider unity of education. Dance and song, the two art-forms which are fairest and most delight God, are to form the chief element in the education of the citizens, and are to lend their amusing power to invest the serious duties of life with that cheerful spontaneity which man shows most of all in his amusements. They are to be used to instil an ethical content into the growing body and mind, and will receive a solemn consecration from the authorities in the State, while artists will only create what is in accordance with the beliefs of the State. Art is to become religious, or, in the language of the *Laws*, what is conventionally held to be a pastime is to be transformed into something serious, though it is still to keep an element of joy in its composition.

Having, then, discussed the position of art with regard to man and State, let us consider a matter that is closely connected with it in Plato's thought at this time, namely, the idea that man is God's plaything. What does this mean from the social point of view, which is, after all, the central preoccupation of the *Laws*? How far can man and State in other than strictly artistic activities be considered as the plaything of God? What religious and theological views does it presuppose?

No one can read the *Laws* without being struck

IN PLATO'S 'LAWS'

by the sudden appearance of this belief that man is God's plaything ($\pi\alpha\iota\gamma\nu\iota o\nu$). It is introduced quite early in the first book in a well-known passage, comparing the conduct of human beings under the influence of various motives to the play of marionettes.

> May we not regard every living being as a puppet of the Gods, which may be their plaything only, or may be created with a purpose ; for that is a matter which we cannot certainly know ? but this we know, that these affections in us are like cords and strings, which pull us different and opposite ways, and to opposite actions ; and herein lies the difference between virtue and vice. The argument tells me that every man ought to follow one of these cords and not let go, but pull with that against all the rest ; and this is the sacred and golden cord of reason, called by us the common law of the State ; there are others also which are hard and of iron, but this is soft because golden ; and there are various other kinds. Now we ought always to co-operate with the lead of the best, which is law. For inasmuch as reason is beautiful and gentle and not violent, her rule must needs have ministers in order to help the golden principle in vanquishing the other principles. . . .[1]

It reappears on page 803, where Plato expounds at length his opinion that amusement and earnestness are identical ; and it is never far distant from his thoughts in the many places where reference is

[1] 644 D (Jowett).

AN ASPECT OF EDUCATION

made to σπουδή and παιδιά. The passage in Book VII. is so striking that it may be given in full :

I say that about serious matters a man should be serious, and about a matter which is not serious he should not be serious ; and that God is the natural and worthy object of man's most serious and blessed endeavours, and that man, as I said before, is made to be the plaything of God, and that this, truly considered, is the best of him ; wherefore every man and woman should follow in this way, and pass life in the noblest of pastimes, and be of another mind from what they now are. Now they think that their serious pursuits should be for the sake of their sports, for they deem war a serious pursuit, which must be managed well for the sake of peace ; but the truth is that there neither is, nor has been, nor ever will be either amusement or instruction in any degree worth speaking of in war, which is nevertheless deemed by us to be the most serious of our pursuits. And, therefore, as we say, every man of us should live the life of peace as long and as well as he can. And what is the right way of living ? Are we to live in sports [1] always ? If so, in what kind of sports ? We ought to live sacrificing and singing and dancing, and then a man will be able to propitiate the Gods, and to defend himself against his enemies and conquer them in battle.[2]

---

[1] Jowett translates παιδιά by sports ; I have used pastime or amusement, because 'sport' has now become too narrow a word to give the full sense of the Greek.

[2] 803 (Jowett).

IN PLATO'S 'LAWS'

The opinion that man is God's plaything, and may not have been put together in earnestness, sounds very different from the views that Plato developed in his earlier works about the dignity of man as 'the spectator of all time and existence,' and on the surface bears a tinge of pessimism not unnatural in one who had met so many disappointments in experience. Sometimes it sounds like the echo of a voice from the New Comedy meditating with a melancholy pathos on the vicissitudes of life. But a careful reading of the *Laws* gives little reason to think that Plato had become pessimistic with advancing years, unless to be practical and to care for ordinary men and women, to be sensible of the possibility of failure, and of the necessity to accept something less than the ideal, if anything is to be achieved, is to be pessimistic. It more probably represents a renunciation of the sovereign claims of dialectic to explain reality, and a final conviction that for the mass of citizens in a State God must remain past finding out, and that it is unnecessary for man to demand or to attempt a justification of all the difficulties of human life from his partial standpoint. God's rule is to be an article of faith and must be accepted in a spirit of religious acquiescence in his wisdom and goodness.

On the basis, then, of this supposition that man is God's plaything, a very definite relationship between man and God is established. As his

AN ASPECT OF EDUCATION

plaything man's final end is to please his Creator, and he thus possesses a standard by which to order the whole of his life. And by declaring that dance and song and sacrifice are the pastimes most welcome to God, Plato shows us what is the form and essence of any human activity that God may find acceptable in his playthings. For these pastimes or amusements are not games in the ordinary signification of the word. Games are distinguished from artistic ' amusements ' by the absence of regularity; they cannot be repeated or fixed in an unchanging form; on the other hand, dance and song and sacrifice are all marked by the presence in them of a very definite form, eliminating from them, as far as possible, the element of chance and variation which is so prominent in games. This definite form may be considered as the serious or earnest element in a work of art, for it is that by which it affects the participator—for instance, in a choric dance—or the spectator. Now this definite form in a work of art is given to it by the artist, and is the mark in it of his reason, distinguishing art from the indeterminate play of children or animals. But there is also an important element that is common both to games and artistic pastimes : it is the spontaneous joy that is aroused by them, in which there is no calculation of utility or ulterior purpose, but a complete satisfaction in the pleasure of the moment and a strong natural instinct to seek it ;

IN PLATO'S 'LAWS'

the participation in such a pastime is accompanied by a sense of physical and mental well-being, which shows it to be in accordance with man's real nature. How strongly Plato felt about the effect of such form as can be imparted even to the 'childish' games of the young is shown by a passage in the seventh book,[1] where he earnestly deprecates any alterations or innovations in the established games, as tending to produce an unstable character in the young, and to weaken the element of 'earnestness' in them, which is subsequently to be so important in those pastimes, which really are the best and fairest for men and most pleasing to God. Dance, song, and sacrifice are conspicuous among serious pastimes by the manifestation of reasoned form in them; they are almost entirely controlled by man, who can therefore make them more rational than any of his ordinary works, in which the intractability of matter and chance forces are felt. The world of artistic creation is largely withdrawn from such accidents, and it must be by virtue of this peculiar fortune that it is the fairest pastime for God's playthings. The play of reason is that which he most delights to see.

In the passage with which I began this discussion we are said to be 'playthings' because we respond so readily to the 'pull' of desires and motives; but there is one wire only to which we

[1] 797.

AN ASPECT OF EDUCATION

ought to respond always, and that is the common law of the city ($κοινὸς\ νόμος$). It is by obedience to the 'pull' of this wire that we present an agreeable pastime to our Creator, and thus the law is the medium by which connection with him is established. Law is for Plato simply the unfolding of reason in the various departments of human life, to produce a recognised regularity of form. Now, the peculiarity of the three 'pastimes' of song, dance, and sacrifice is the permanence of form given them by the presence of rational law, and the immediate enjoyment arising from participation in them; but it now appears that this peculiarity of form is not confined to them alone, for there are other activities of man—for instance, his social and political duties where law is the informing power—though, in general, they are not regarded in the same way as the artistic activities, because they are held to have their purpose beyond themselves in some social or political ideal to be achieved in the future. Remembering, then, that man is God's plaything by his obedience to the 'pull' of divine law, must we not consider that political and social duties are also pastimes for God's playthings to perform, in the same manner as those artistic activities which are in themselves purely pleasurable? Does Plato intend any distinction to be made between the political and artistic forms of activity within the State?

This suggested assimilation of political to artistic forms of experience is also supported by a mode of thought that is very characteristic of the *Laws*. Throughout the whole work Plato contends, sometimes in jest, sometimes in earnest, against the customary division of life into things serious or amusing. In his commentary on the *Laws*, Ritter [1] has collected together all the passages in which the opposition or identity of the two terms (σπουδή παιδιά, παίζειν) occurs, and his results show that beneath great diversity and difficulty of content this particular opinion rests upon a sure foundation. How are we to distinguish playfulness from seriousness, Plato seems to ask, in a world where man is the plaything of heaven? Let us be on the safe side and treat our play seriously and our serious things playfully, always remembering what the true pattern of play is. And if we follow out this idea one great benefit will result. Those serious political duties which seemed, especially to the citizen of the fourth century B.C., irksome and devoid of pleasure, would be undertaken in the willing and happy spirit of his pastimes. That is the ideal at which Plato is aiming; the old dualistic attitude to life is to be broken down, and there is to be no distinction between the enjoyment of pastimes and duties. The common element of both is the reasonable form, in which both choric dance and,

[1] Ritter, *Platos Gesetze. Kommentar.*, p. 15 *seq.*

for instance, military service are presented and accepted. All political duties, in proportion as they are penetrated by reason, become more and more a free creation of man, approximating to the artistic creation of song or dance : never in quite so free or spiritual a manner, because the unreasonable element of matter and chance enters more into the composition of a State, but always able to afford man pleasure in following out, as in a true pastime, the orderly movement of reason or law. It is in accordance with this idea of political life, as a creation formed by reason, and having its own delight in itself, that Plato prefixes to all his laws an appeal for obedience, based on the rational or 'serious' element in man, and does not present them as categoric imperatives. In the general preface to the code the man who excels in obedience to the laws through all his life is to be extolled above the victors in any Olympic game or contest of peace or war.[1] Nor is simple obedience enough : there must be a willingness to check or to make known to those in authority the wickedness of others, and to assist them in the execution of the laws. This is the fullest exercise of reasonable law to which the individual can attain, preventing him from aiming at any isolated perfection, and drawing him body and soul into the great unity of society. Thus it is clear why Plato takes choric dance and sacrifice as the two

[1] 729 D.

noblest forms of pastime. Choric dance as an art-form is different from what we, in general, expect a work of art to be : we look for something that stands in isolation, as an object to a contemplating subject—for instance, a statue, a picture, or a piece of music. For Plato the noblest art-forms are those in which there is community of performance and enjoyment, so that man experiences its charm not in isolation, but in expansion of life with his fellows ; employed educationally they are to make more easy the acceptance, as pastimes, of those activities which men now regard erroneously as serious—that is, containing no pleasure in them.

Thus man's ordinary life, and the life of the State as a whole, should be viewed as a pastime performed in the service of God by his playthings. It is the most serious thing for man, because his particular temporal existence depends on its successful performance ; but he cannot perform it successfully unless he enters into it in the spirit of play, finding complete satisfaction in the actual performance and expecting nothing beyond it. And God approves of it, just as he approved of song and dance and sacrifice, because their essence is law, and all the law of the universe is only his will and is but the unfolding of his own nature.

Again, this assertion of the identity of earnestness and pastime or amusement renders Plato's general criticism of art much more comprehensible and justifiable. The accepted convention about art was that it came into existence simply to amuse, and that the artist was bound by no laws, but was inspired in some mysterious way to do his work. Plato resented the idea that anything so powerful as art could exercise its influence without proper knowledge in its creator of his intention and the means by which to achieve that intention. In the *Republic* and in the *Laws* he legislates against artists, who claim a God-given inspiration and freedom to say whatever they like. Art was no less divine to him than it was to those inspired artists of whom he was so frightened, but for him the essence of divinity in anything was the acknowledgment and expression of law, and the art whose form was not moulded by law appeared to him dangerous to the State and in opposition to the will of God. And with this conviction of the rational form of art must, of necessity, go the belief that it was not idle amusement. Whatever can show, in the slightest degree, the working of law within itself has a serious quality, and art according to Plato's belief should show in the most perfect manner, though in but a small part of man's total activity, the domination of law. The rest of his life must aspire to that condition, and, wherever a perfect code of law is devised and obeyed by the citizens, there the State becomes a grand work of art. The great value of art is that in it

God has given man an example of how the whole of his life may be made perfect and acceptable to him. The true function of art is to be the educator of the citizens—Plato risks a pun on the resemblance between παιδιά and παιδεία—and the giver of joy to society in its serious occupations. That spirit of joy which is characteristic of all amusement, whether children's games or the more serious games of art, is to be diffused everywhere; the austere and self-sacrificing air of duty is to be replaced by that spirit of joy and charity which was so conspicuous in the early Christians, and whose presence in this ideal State makes us feel that, if such a society could be realised, it would be more akin to a 'church militant' than to any political State. It is that spirit alone which can make tolerable the minute prescriptions of the *Laws*.

It is curious that Plato did not make use of this apparent opposition of earnestness and play in considering the relationship of soul and body in God's playthings. After God, soul, as being most akin to him, is the most divine thing in the world, and therefore comes next to him as an object of earnestness for man. It is man's duty to honour his soul truly, and not in the false manner of those who claim to do so while serving only their body, and its good is to be preferred before all the attractions of wealth or beauty or strength, which are 'physical goods.' The body is only to be taken

AN ASPECT OF EDUCATION

seriously so far as it can assist in the development of the ' divine goods ' ; it is that with which the ordinary games of children are played, while the fine play of man is that orderly service of God in which the soul indulges as mistress of herself and of her body. Such is the line of thought that Plato's general attitude would suggest, and it is certainly in accordance with the pronounced opposition he establishes between soul and body, allowing no serious consideration of the body by itself, much less any equality in honour.

> We must believe the legislator when he tells us that the soul is in all respects superior to the body, and that even in life what makes each one of us to be what we are is only the soul ; and the body follows us about in the likeness of each of us, and therefore, when we are dead, the bodies of the dead are rightly said to be our shades or images. . . .[1]

That warfare between soul and body, which is so insisted upon in the teaching of Christianity, is already an established fact in the thought of Plato. This teaching of the identity of σπουδή and παιδιά in the unification of man's activities is not unworthy of Plato's genius. It is an attempt to exchange the severe endeavour to obey the law and to serve the State for joyful participation and co-operation in the play of life. And it is thus that Plato describes the life of his State when

[1] 959 (Jowett), 828 D, ' The connection of soul and body is no way better than the dissolution of them, as I am ready to maintain quite seriously.'

meeting the appeal of dramatic poets to be allowed to give representations in the city. By these means he hoped to widen the power of his appeal to men ; the beauty of the moral law, the intellectual love of God, are pleasures too austere to win the obedience of the rank and file of the citizens who exercise a tremendous influence in the State. Play or amusement, on the other hand, is something that is familiar to all, that exercises its power, whether as idle amusement or artistic enjoyment ; it is, too, something that is pursued for its own sake without self-sacrifice to a distant end. These are two qualities of play which Plato wishes to use : firstly, the willingness of the performer, and secondly, the performing of the play for its own sake. He hopes to bring into man's political life a combination of rationality and pleasure so as to secure his entire devotion to realising the ideal. It is not, therefore, difficult to understand why little definite teaching about immortality, or even the hope of a personal future existence, is given in the *Laws*. That would defeat the main object of Plato's effort, which is to make this life a play that is really earnest and self-sufficient. The living of life according to the laws of divine reason is the eternal life, something that is being perpetually enjoyed, and brings the highest happiness with it ; it is the same life that is being lived more perfectly by the visible gods in heaven, the sun and moon, the

AN ASPECT OF EDUCATION

planets and stars, and by the great Creator of all things, who 'journeys for ever along the undeviating path of divine law.'[1] If there is any after-life for man, it is only a transference to some better or worse place, according to the laws of unchanging justice, to attempt afresh the play of life; there is no suggestion of the survival of personal consciousness. The general outlines of that after-life Plato leaves vague, only emphasising very clearly the absolute certainty of judgment for all alike on the deeds of the life they have finished.

> This is divine justice which neither you nor any other unfortunate will ever glory in escaping, and which the ordaining powers have specially ordained; take good heed of them, for a day will come when they will take heed of you. If you say: I am small and will creep into the depths of the earth, or I am high and will fly up to heaven, you are not so small or so high but that you shall pay the fitting penalty, either in the world below or in some yet more savage place to which you shall be conveyed.[2]

It now remains to form some idea about the nature of the God who contrives this play.

In the fourth book, 716 C, the question is asked: ' What kind of conduct is welcome and obedient to the will of God?' The answer is given, that God is the measure to which all things must be referred; that the man who would be dear to him must resemble him as far as possible by

[1] 716.   [2] 904-5 (Jowett).

IN PLATO'S 'LAWS'

obedience to law, which is the spirit of moderation (σώφρων), and avoidance of all injustice or evil, which is wilful disregard of law. In 713 E man is told to obey the immortal principle that is in him; this immortal or divine principle is given to him by the distribution of reason (διανομὴ τοῦ νοῦ) and is known as law (νόμος). (Plato cannot resist the temptation to support his argument by a playful appeal to the resemblance in root of the three words.) God alone has this immortal principle of reason in its fullest and purest form; his mind is the rational order of the universe. The other element of his nature is soul (ψυχή), that which is prior to matter [1] and is the source of all movement or actualisation of law. From him man has received a portion of these two elements, so that he recognises the value of law and can exercise himself in it. God is always accompanied by the spirit of justice,[2] who corrects all disobedience to the divine law. Plato is at pains to show that this justice [3] is very different from human justice, for God can never be induced to deviate from his course by human prayer or sacrifice. This supreme God has created [4] and upholds the universe in the manner of an artist; he alone contemplates the whole and can see the justice of each thing's part in it. The whole is, on a grander scale, similar to that which man performs on his small stage of state, receiving its

[1] 898-9. [2] 716 A. [3] 905, 599. [4] 903.

power of movement (ψυχή) from him, as well as the law according to which it moves. But the Creator is not the only divine being in the universe, though he is the highest; the sun and moon and planets and stars are also gods, deities ever visible to the eye of man to sustain his faith, while the Creator is only to be grasped by the mind. The divinity of these heavenly bodies rests on the complete rationality of their movement; the soul that is in them experiences no resistance to its law. Plato considers it to be the greatest impiety to accuse the heavenly bodies of irregularity in their movements, and intends his citizens to have enough knowledge of astronomy to counteract such wrong ideas. The perfection of their orderliness is the ideal which man should strive to realise, to which he approximates most nearly in song and dance, and the happiness of the world, as of the smaller human society, consists in this voluntary fulfilment of law. Thus Plato can find no higher relationship to express the life of the gods and the control of the universe by the Creator than that contained in the ideal of human art. The dance of the stars is divine, because chance or disobedience to law is excluded from it; it is the most perfect spectacle for the Creator. In human life chance and opportunity as well as God hold sway,[1] but art reduces to narrow limits the action of chance, banishing it almost entirely from true

[1] 709.

artistic creations, and making its effect less and less noticeable in political and social creations, in proportion as men establish the true form of reality, which is law, in those spheres of life.

From all this it is surely clear that the statement that man is God's plaything does not imply anything contemptuous about man's position in the universe, nor does it mean that each individual is an isolated or meaningless puppet in God's hand. There is undoubtedly a note of sorrow in Plato's utterance at the end of his life that we have little knowledge of the truth ;[1] all the more does he insist on the necessity of religious faith. The plaything has its true existence in the unity of society, for there alone can the pull of 'common' law be felt ; and the play is nothing but their co-ordinated movement according to law. Similarly in religion the highest ideal is κοινὰ τὰ τῶν φιλῶν; the individual enters most deeply into relationship with God in his union with other men. 'No man shall have sacred rites in a private house. But when he is disposed to sacrifice, let him place his offerings in the hands of the priests and priestesses who have under their care the holy rite, and let him pray himself, and let any one who pleases join with him in prayer.'[2] In those words he is not very far in spirit from the saying of Jesus : 'Where two or three are gathered together in my name, there am I in the midst of them.'

[1] 804 B.   [2] 909 (Jowett).

THE CLASSIC PASTORAL AND GIORGIONE

EVERY visitor to the picture-galleries of the Louvre has seen, consciously or unconsciously, the picture by Giorgione called 'La Fête Champêtre,' if only for the reason that it now hangs beside Da Vinci's 'Mona Lisa,' the best-known and most visited picture in Europe. And in this position it makes a fine contrast to the mysterious lady of Leonardo's imagination, so inscrutable and superior in expression and form that Walter Pater's eloquence does not really persuade us that she is what 'men in the ways of a thousand years had come to desire.' How much more simple and direct is the appeal of Giorgione's picture, where in the full light of a Venetian summer day a group of men and women are gathered together in the shade by a well to make music. Once a brilliant star in the galaxy of masterpieces which decorated the walls of the Salle Carrée in days before the war, 'La Fête Champêtre' has now been transferred, together with Leonardo's 'Mona Lisa' and 'St. Anne' and a few favoured Titians and Correggios, to a Tribuna which breaks the endless vista of the Long Gallery. And there amid the other masterpieces of the full Renaissance this work triumphantly abides all comparison, not only by splendour

THE CLASSIC PASTORAL AND GIORGIONE

of colour and beauty of painting, but because it presents in imaginative form an ideal of life constantly recurring in the history of civilisation since our primitive forefathers ceased from their nomadic existence and began the long process of civilised life in villages and cities. And this picture has also won for itself a second kind of immortality by finding an interpreter of its spirit in the poet Dante Gabriel Rossetti.

In general, poems upon pictures are but the pale reflections of bright originals, belonging to the world of descriptive culture rather than of art. To communicate by words the significance of a picture is beyond the power of any poet, for the final effect of each art is inextricably involved in its own peculiar medium of expression. This sonnet by Rossetti is the most successful of such ventures, because the work which he interprets combines in a perfect balance illustrative and decorative qualities, and is inspired by a feeling for the preciousness of poetry and music in life. And in the appreciation of such a moment the poet's delicate insight and gift of language may enable us to perceive better than we could do for ourselves the fullness of its illustrative genius, and intensify our enjoyment of it as a work of art.

Water, for anguish of the solstice :—nay,
    But dip the vessel slowly,—nay, but lean
    And hark how at its verge the wave sighs in

THE CLASSIC PASTORAL AND GIORGIONE

Reluctant. Hush ! Beyond all depth away
The heat lies silent at the brink of day ;
    Now the hand trails upon the viol string
    That sobs, and the brown faces cease to sing,
Sad with the whole of pleasure. Whither stray
Her eyes now, from whose mouth the slim pipes creep
    And leave it pouting, while the shadowed grass
    Is cool against her naked side ? Let be :—
Say nothing now unto her lest she weep,
    Nor name this ever. Be it as it was,—
    Life touching lips with immortality.

Rossetti has entitled his sonnet ' For a Venetian Pastoral by Giorgione,' and the word ' pastoral ' inevitably carries the mind back to the earlier manifestations of the pastoral in European art. His great predecessors in this style are not painters but poets, and, in spite of the immense popularity of pastoral poetry in Italy during the fifteenth century, nothing had been produced which could in any way shake the supremacy of Virgil and Theocritus. With the revival of Greek learning, Theocritus was born again into the world as a direct influence and model, now capable of being clearly distinguished from his curious reflection in Virgil's *Eclogues*. Virgil, on the other hand, was the one poet of antiquity whose fate it had been to live on in continuous activity from the ancient through the mediæval into the modern world, as poet and prophet, a spirit naturally Christian, who had entered by countless ways into the general

THE CLASSIC PASTORAL AND GIORGIONE

consciousness of the civilisation of the Renaissance. We cannot, of course, put our fingers on this or that detail in Giorgione's work and say that it shows the direct influence of Virgil or Theocritus. We know little enough about the painter's life, still less about his education and the associations of his short career. He must, as a finely gifted nature, have been very susceptible to the richness and variety of Venetian life at the end of the fifteenth century, with its unique combination of the sea and mainland, and the remains of his art express that peculiar moment when life, secure in all that it has won for itself from the past, becomes conscious of its own goodness, and desires to have that feeling presented to itself in concrete form. And it is the complete seriousness and harmonious presentation of such an ideal in this picture as something final, which is the measure of the difference between the Venetian and all other expressions of the pastoral spirit, breathing into it the passion which is wanting in Theocritus and the unity which is wanting in Virgil's early work.

The scenery of the Venetian and Lombardy plains is generally considered to be an uninspiring stretch of agricultural land, devoid of beauty or romance in the eyes of the modern tourist on his way to Venice or Central Italy. Yet it is to artists born and brought up in these districts that we owe the most satisfying and poetical treatment of the Italian landscape in the true pastoral sense.

THE CLASSIC PASTORAL AND GIORGIONE

Mantua, Correggio and Castelfranco, the birthplace of Giorgione, rather than the Venetian Alps and the mountainous scenery of Central Italy, have moulded the eyes and minds which have wrought out most successfully the truly permanent and pervasive forms of nature on which alone true intimacy of feeling can be established. Archæologists have not yet decided, and without the appearance of fresh facts there seems no hope that they ever will be able to decide with certainty, the locality of Virgil's farm. Nor, indeed, is it a matter of much importance. Whether it lay to the east of Mantua near Pietole, or to the north-west at Calvisano, as some recent scholars suggest, the immediate physical nature of the land and the distant horizon of northern Alps would be the same. Verona, the most important town to the north of this district, is only fifty miles west of Castelfranco, and though Mantua, properly speaking, is outside the Venetian province, the tradition exists in ancient grammarians that Virgil was of Venetian stock, possibly on his mother's side. And there is much to support this tradition in the similarity with which both artists, essentially imaginative and meditative temperaments, reacted to the landscape and the business of country life which surrounded them during the years of their development.

The level and fertile fields which stretch in all directions round Mantua, bounded on the north

THE CLASSIC PASTORAL AND GIORGIONE

by the line of the distant Alps, bear much resemblance to that district of the mainland north of Venice in which Castelfranco lies. Venetia seems a little more luxuriant, the sheltering barrier of the Alps a little nearer, but in both places there is the same bounteousness of earth, inviting man to active work upon it and to quiet enjoyment of its delights. It is a landscape in which the grander effects of nature are wanting : the Alps are too far away to be a dominating influence ; the big rivers flow down into the Po or the sea unobserved, and the serene air and perfect lines of the hills in Umbria and Tuscany are altogether wanting in Lombardy. There are no romantic elements in this landscape, and neither Arcadia nor Sicily has anything to show more strictly pastoral than the scenery in which Virgil and Giorgione grew up. Yet the relationship between pastoral scenery and the pastoral as a form of art is by no means simple. The artist is more than a photographer of his surroundings, and the work which he finally gives to the world is not the form in which reality first came to his eyes, but a fusion of external things with the forms of his imagination effected by the fire of emotion—that is, by temperamental qualities. And, in view of their greatness, it is not without interest to see how Virgil and Giorgione, familiar with the same kind of landscape and country life, sprung perhaps from the same stock of people, and creative at the same

THE CLASSIC PASTORAL AND GIORGIONE

age, have used the pastoral theme as a significant mode of self-expression.

Virgil is not the founder of the pastoral, though with him it may be said to have been born again, for he, rather than Theocritus, has been the dominant influence in the development of the pastoral in European literature. It is traditional in literary criticism to consider Virgil's *Eclogues* as closely modelled upon the work of Theocritus, and critics and commentators of those poems have too often succeeded in transforming the *Eclogues* into variations in a minor key upon the finer themes of the Greek poet. All through these poems we continually meet with motives taken from Theocritus, thoughts and lines and half-lines translated literally into Latin. Yet in the final result the debt is seen to be purely nominal, and the pattern which Virgil has woven with this borrowed material is utterly different from the original. In the process of translation the plumes have become dyed with Virgilian colours; they have suffered in their passage across the Sicilian sea ' a change into something rich and strange,' so that any attempt to judge the Virgilian pastoral by the standard of Theocritus's work must end in misapprehension and disappointment.

> Theocritus [writes Mr. Mackail in his book on Greek poetry] is the first and greatest of the pastoral poets. . . . In him the pastoral became classic, and that was the last transmutation which

THE CLASSIC PASTORAL AND GIORGIONE

the spirit of poetry took fully and with complete success in Greek hands before she passed westward from the Greek world.

In the single word 'classic' the vital difference between Theocritus and Virgil is completely expressed. For though Theocritus lived when the flower of free life in the cities of Greece had faded into the formless monotony of Alexandrian civilisation, he possesses by a peculiar gift the earlier and essential artistic qualities of the Greeks, their objective vision, their flawless unity and simplicity of subject. His mastery over the technique of formal presentation is perfect, and the fascination of that technique so great, that every mode of pastoral life which he handles seems to stand before us as a permanent model. He is 'classic' in the narrower or conventional signification of the word by which the great writers of Greece are thought to be inordinately occupied with the creation of severe and impersonal form. But the poets and prose writers of the sixth and fifth centuries B.C. are classical in the deeper and truer meaning of the word; they rest upon the central issues of life, and the true classical writers of Greece are those in whom art and life are co-extensive, who are dominated as citizens no less than as artists by the desire to give satisfactory form to life as the all-absorbing and sole activity of man.

The change which came over the world with the establishment of Macedonian power in Greece

THE CLASSIC PASTORAL AND GIORGIONE

completely altered the relationship of State and individual. The old unity of life was broken, and with it of necessity was broken the unity of art as an interpretation of that life ; nor has that unity ever again been re-established. As the conquests of Alexander became consolidated into various kingdoms the age of the professional classes began, when the mass of men in cities, freed from most political and military duties, were occupied with the gaining of their livelihood in business, and the variety of individual experience was immensely narrowed. A contrast arose between the business life, with its times of leisure and amusement when a man wished to be ' taken out of himself,' and the other forms of life in the world outside his city of which he had no experience. And here it was that art, entirely released from her service to the State, came forward to relieve the tedium and restrictions of the monotonous city life by holding up the image of other forms of life, showing first one and then another of the facets into which the clear uniformity of the old Hellenic life had been cut. When the city dweller wished for an extension of his horizon, artists were not slow in presenting to him scenes of high adventure and romance in strange and distant lands, or, with an equally welcome contrast, humble scenes of country life in which shepherds and herdsmen express in naïve or quaint fashion the common joys and sorrows and interests of men. The

THE CLASSIC PASTORAL AND GIORGIONE

creation and perfecting of these pastoral poems is the peculiar glory of Theocritus, ' the last poet among the Greek classics,' facing both ways, like Janus, towards the earlier poets of Greece in virtue of his form, towards Virgil and the world of modern poetry by the quality of his subject-matter.

The charm of Theocritus is that of selected moments. Over most of the idylls, at least the most popular ones, there is spread an atmosphere of dramatic self-consciousness, due, no doubt, to the influence of the popular Sicilian *mime*, or dramatic sketch, whose realism is touched by no finer purpose than the presentation of a quaint or piquant situation, and is sometimes satisfied by the direct reproduction in verse of the conversation of shepherds. Just as the pastoral poem itself is short, so the action represented is short without extension to past or future, taking that life, not at its own most significant value, but at a moment which may appeal to others by its difference from their own mode of life, and by the absence of all those more serious issues or mysterious moments which bring home to us both the beauty and the pathos of things. The passages in the pastoral life which Theocritus selects are for the most part only true to nature or life in a secondary degree ; they interpret, not the country life over which trouble and toil and uncertainty are always imminent, but a certain aspect of the consciousness of the city dweller, not wholly

THE CLASSIC PASTORAL AND GIORGIONE

satisfied with his own mode of existence and seeking distraction in the choice moments of a different life, where the emotions of ordinary humanity are shown in fanciful and novel characters and in musical surroundings. Consider, for instance, the famous poems on the love of the Cyclops Polyphemus for Galatea. The traditional figure of the bloodthirsty giant is presented as a youth still living with his mother, undergoing the fancies and pangs of first love. His uncouth face and huge force disappear in the gentle sentimentality of his love ; his strength is used to gather flowers and train animals to be the pets of Galatea. He is playful and fanciful as he sits upon the rocky shore making music to his thoughts, waiting for his loved one to appear, while behind him on the sloping pastures his flocks feed, and above the rocks and woods of the higher ground is seen the snowy summit of Etna. The charm of these poems lies in the unexpected association of many slight but essentially human characteristics in the mind of this externally strange creature, sensitive, vain, truthful, and sincere, so strong and yet a child in the hands of Love. And in the same kind of poetry we must include the highly-finished serenade (Idyll III.), where the love-sick shepherd enchants us by the perfection of his verse harmonising so admirably with the delicate curiosity of each succeeding fancy, so that the touches of rustic realism and the beauty of mythological

THE CLASSIC PASTORAL AND GIORGIONE

legend, as in the sequence of a dream, cease for the moment to be incongruous. And in the purely pastoral idylls, where the quaint or fanciful has no place, we do not find any depth in the feeling for nature, anything beyond the immediate sensuous and physical enjoyment of sunlight and shade, of murmuring breezes and rippling water. It is the mirror-like reflection of perfect weather. The travellers' songs are heard in the cloudless heat of midday when the lizard is asleep on the wall, and even the birds have ceased to sing ; then from the heat and brightness of the open road they pass into the orchard of Phrasidemus, and rest in the long grass beneath the fruit trees whose laden boughs bend to the earth, while the air all round is filled with the murmurings of grasshoppers and bees and doves. The scene is almost too rich, too much like the dream of one who has been 'long in city pent,' yet this is perhaps the only idyll in which the poet is himself moved by the memory, as he was by the actual experience, of a day of untroubled felicity and complete physical well-being, in which the process of life disappears from consciousness, and he prays to Demeter, whose statue stood close beside the threshing-floor of Phrasidemus :

> May I oft again
> Set up my shovel in her golden heap,
> While she with radiant bounty beaming holds
> Poppies and sheaves of corn in either hand.[1]

---

[1] Idyll vii. ; trans. Kynaston.

THE CLASSIC PASTORAL AND GIORGIONE

For the truth is that the pastoral poetry of Theocritus is not an interpretation of life, not even of the pastoral life. The time was past when life could be viewed either steadily or whole. His poetry is rather a refuge from life, something that holds the attention and charms the thoughts without stirring the emotions, realistic in detail without touching the deeper reality of the country and life in it. How often the empty adjectives 'sweet' and 'beautiful' do duty for all determination of content, expressing the simple and immediate enjoyment of fine weather, of the breeze heard in the trees, of rippling water on hot days, of the freshness of the sea, delights as fragile as the verse in which they are described, which the first cloud, or the first chill of autumn, will dispel, for they are presented without relationship to the more permanent and intimate interests of life.

To turn from the pastorals of Theocritus to those of Virgil is in some degree to repeat Alice's experience of passing through the looking-glass. The figures and phrases of the conventional pastoral are there, but their relationships are utterly different. It is not simply that Virgil is a Roman and Theocritus a Greek poet. Virgil is different from any Roman poet. Lucretius may be as great, perhaps a greater, poet; the greatness of Virgil rests on his being something more than a great Roman poet. He is the last great poet of the ancient world, reaching out by some mysteri-

THE CLASSIC PASTORAL AND GIORGIONE

ous quality of thought and language, due perhaps to the North Italian or Venetian blood in his veins, from the ancient into the modern world.

> Last in the train of night
> If better thou belong not to the dawn.

And it was from him that, thirteen hundred years after his death, Dante received the torch of poetry, spreading the grace of Christian sentiment over him by making him his guide through hell and purgatory to the earthly paradise.

The *Eclogues* are the record of Virgil's early inspiration, written before he was much over thirty, with his genius well developed, but by no means at the full height of his powers. There is not a single eclogue that has the unity or objective transparency of Theocritus's *Idylls*. Allegory, erudition, political allusions, inconsistencies of scenery, are all apparent in the *Eclogues*. The rustics, if they are meant to be such, are stiff and artificial without the quaintness or naturalness which are the assets of the Theocritean shepherd. In his external form Virgil is the father of all that artificial pastoral which flourished so abundantly in Italian poetry, and passed from it into the court pastorals and country pleasures of the French painters in the eighteenth century. Yet the qualities which make the poetical magic of the *Georgics* and *Æneid* are present too in the *Eclogues*, illuminating the new motives, the deeper content

THE CLASSIC PASTORAL AND GIORGIONE

which Virgil infuses into the traditional form of the *Eclogues*. His relationship to the country is personal, and carries with it a force of emotion that Theocritus never achieves; the more humble and permanent facts of country life, the varied pageantry of cloud and shadow on hill and plain, make the beauty of song in the midst of nature more real and lasting. Thus at the end of the first eclogue, which is a curious mixture of personal feeling for home and of political allusion with idyllic description and geographical learning, we come suddenly upon two lines of simple observation which bring us back from Augustus and Amaryllis to the eternal process of life and nature, to the smoke which curls up from the cottage in the evening air and to the lengthening of the shadows as the sun sinks behind the western hills.

Et iam summa procul villarum culmina fumant,
maioresque cadunt altis de montibus umbrae.

And, see, the farm roof chimneys smoke afar,
And from the hills the shadows lengthening fall.[1]

And again towards the end of the second eclogue:

The ox comes home
With plough uptilted, and the shadows grow
To twice their length with the departing sun.[2]

And then there is the spell wrought by the transition from the light rhythms and music of Theocritus to the Latin hexameter moulded by the

[1] Trans. Rhodes. [2] *Ibid.*

THE CLASSIC PASTORAL AND GIORGIONE

art of Virgil. The beauty, for instance, of the last eclogue or of the famous poem to Pollio lies in the variety and depth of the verbal music harmonising the strange collocations, the actual and ideal, into the delight of song in and for itself, a constant delight, too, in poetical colour, in richness of language and rhythm, existing also in the *Georgics* and *Æneid*, but in a much more subdued form, as though advancing years and the scenery of the South had chastened that serene and luxuriant imagery which has shown itself again and again in the history of art as the peculiar possession of artists from the plains of Lombardy and Venetia. It distinguishes Catullus and Livy, natives of Verona and Padua ; it is the transcendent dower of the great Venetian painters of the fifteenth and sixteenth centuries, so that it may not be entirely fanciful to trace in the pastoral pictures of Giorgione and his school a reminiscence or a reincarnation of the spirit of the Virgilian pastoral. For the *Eclogues* of Virgil present, not the pastoral life as a moment of amusement or distraction, but as a certain ideal of civilised life, the passionate enjoyment of music, with others, in a favoured spot on a summer day when men, fatigued with the endless series of practical affairs, hope to realise all the possibilities of life, of which they are now conscious, the harmony of inner and outer beauty in the happy union of art and nature.

O mihi tum longae maneat pars ultima vitae.

THE CLASSIC PASTORAL AND GIORGIONE

In 1495 the printer Aldus published at Venice the *editio princeps* of Theognis in which were included thirty poems of Theocritus. Giorgione must have been in Venice then or shortly afterwards. Born at Castelfranco in 1478, he went to Venice to study painting in the studio of Giovanni Bellini, and it is very probable that he may have heard translations of some of the idylls at the musical festivals of those distinguished personages with whom Vasari says he was so popular on account of his musical talent. The simple beauty of Theocritus's seventh idyll, with its songs and scenes of harvest happiness, would have impressed an artist's imagination, and the first idea of the ' Fête Champêtre ' may have been founded upon some echo of the Sicilian poet. But, though the idea of the picture may have arisen in this way, the elaboration of this masterpiece, and of all the school of Venetian pastoral, has nothing of the peculiar qualities of Greek or even Alexandrian art. The style of Giorgione's painting is entirely derived from the traditions of the Venetian school, or, more narrowly considered, it is an adaptation or enlargement of his master's teaching in the service of a new ideal. In the ' Madonna Enthroned ' at Castelfranco, the chief surviving specimen of his treatment of religious subject-matter, we can perceive at once the working of a new motive in the way in which he reduces the values of the figures to the scale and tone of the serene land-

THE CLASSIC PASTORAL AND GIORGIONE

scape, while in his pastorals we can feel how much he has carried on from the solemn intensity of Giovanni Bellini's colour. Giorgione died in 1510, thirty-two years old, six years before the death of Bellini, yet between the work of master and pupil lies the discovery of a new world. Man has discovered himself, has discovered the beauty of the world and the beauty of art, and it is Giorgione who has left us the typical expression of this discovery in pictorial form, in the 'Shepherd Boy' at Hampton Court, listening to and enjoying the melody of his music after the actual sounds have died away, and still more fully in the 'Fête Champêtre.'

This picture marks a new moment in the history of painting, the appearance in the fullness of perfection, sudden and mysterious as the birth of Athena from the head of Zeus, of a new kind of art-form. It may be the strange suddenness of this apparition which has caused some critics to take away this picture from Giorgione and give it to a painter of later date, although no one has succeeded in finding a painter whose temperament and surroundings and upbringing would render his claim to this work more persuasive. With it the life of the pastoral in painting begins and at once reaches maturity; no further development of this spirit, only variations upon it, are possible, and those variations we find in the other pictures which are generally assigned to the author of this work, such as the landscape in the Giovanelli Palace at Venice, the 'Venus' of Dresden, and the 'Shepherd Boy' at Hampton Court. Nor is it difficult to find in the work of his master, Giovanni Bellini, premonitions—*splendores antelucani*—of this new creation; his treatment of landscape always shows great feeling for it, and in his later work tends to become something more than the background upon which the figures are placed. That wonderful picture in the Pitti Palace called 'A Sacred Allegory,' where a number of saints are grouped together in contemplation in a splendid landscape, shows his art verging upon the transition which Giorgione made. Given a pupil whose emotional power was deep without being religious in the formal sense, and the transformation of a Sacred Allegory into a Pastoral was easily made. And the figures in Giorgione's 'Fête Champêtre' are no less seriously and intensely absorbed in their music and in the appreciation of the moment than the saints of Giovanni Bellini in their contemplative devotion.

The pastoral in general lacks what Matthew Arnold calls 'high seriousness.' Theocritus never strikes such a note, while it is the presence of this seriousness which makes the pastoral spirit of Giorgione akin to that of Virgil. It is a quality of his colour felt in the whole and in the individual figures and forms of nature, just as it pervades the Virgilian hexameter, passing from these

THE CLASSIC PASTORAL AND GIORGIONE

formal or structural elements into the subject represented and endowing it with a deep significance. And this suggestiveness is the peculiar genius of the Virgilian and Giorgionesque art. The paintings of Jacopo Bassano and many another lesser Venetian, which are conspicuously pastoral in spirit, do not pass beyond the direct beauty of nature and country life. They do not demand a certain relationship to the subject on the part of the spectator. But the appreciation of the *Eclogues* and of Giorgione's work depends upon an intellectual and artistic development of mind, and this dependence is to some degree a limitation of their æsthetic value. They do not work upon our emotions directly by their form or colour in the way in which the frescoes of Michael Angelo or a Romanesque building affect us. Undoubtedly they possess a certain direct beauty of form and colour ; but this was not all that the artist intended to express. He refers deliberately to the emotions of life by expressing in ideal form the highest value which, in his judgment, life can afford, and he counts upon the sympathy of his audience. In this respect his appeal is limited. The *Eclogues* of Virgil are addressed primarily to a circle of poetically gifted men, intimate friends of the writer, eagerly pursuing the art and the delight of poetry, then to a timeless audience who, very sensitive to the beauty of nature and of art, find in this serious pastoral poem or painting the simultaneous satisfaction of those two emotions. That the actual scene depicted by the painter or poet may be far from the experience of that audience is of no account, for it is only the symbol, clear and monumental in proportion to the greatness of the artist, of a whole series of personal emotional experiences. It is this essentially personal element, this reference to a particular experience of art and natural beauty, which makes the limitations of this revelation of the pastoral spirit in Virgil and Giorgione. The illustrative element in such work is too pronounced to allow it to exercise so universal or powerful a sway as the poetry of Homer or the art of Michael Angelo or Titian. It belongs to a refined form of material development when the long process of culture culminates and pauses, as if conscious of its completeness, for a moment of reflection upon itself. Virgil is the focus in which the genius of Italy as well as of Rome is centred. At the age when Giorgione died, Virgil, under the prompting of Augustus and his own patriotic feeling, widened and deepened his artistic form to consider the larger aspects of the country in the *Georgics* and the national significance of Italy in the *Æneid*. And in the same way, Giorgione's life comes at the culmination of Venetian civilisation, when, though her political power was failing, the external splendour and grace of life in Venice were at their highest point. ' It is the most triumphant

THE CLASSIC PASTORAL AND GIORGIONE

city I have ever seen,' wrote Philippe de Comines in 1494. Yet there is a sense of sadness in the comment which both these artists make upon the beauty to be realised in such a life, coming from the same quality of artistic temperament, worked upon by the same local influences, and warmed by the same racial blood.

The delight in noble landscape without his reflective sentiment is transmitted from Giorgione to the great Venetian painters of the sixteenth century, romantically magnificent and vital in Titian and Tintoretto, or unaffectedly pastoral in the best work of Palma Vecchio and the school of Bassano. But the higher pastoral harmony of man and nature could not be recaptured. The curiously meditative standpoint of such pictures as 'The Three Ages of Life' at Bridgewater House and 'Sacred and Profane Love' in the Borghese Gallery at Rome shows how strong was the influence of Giorgione's vision upon the virile genius of Titian. And, externally at least, it was to the narrower form of pastoral that Titian returned in extreme old age, when he painted the wonderful 'Shepherd and Nymph' in the Imperial Gallery at Vienna. But the harmony of music and life and landscape, such as Giorgione knew, is now dispelled. Rocks and broken trees replace the serene summer landscape of the 'Fête Champêtre.' The atmosphere as well as the splendid forms of nymph and shepherd have something tragic about them,

THE CLASSIC PASTORAL AND GIORGIONE

very different from the sadness of 'the whole of pleasure,' as though, for once, the proverb *si jeunesse savait* was reversed and youth knew and was powerless.

It is in the work of Watteau, 'prince of court painters,' that we find again the peculiar pastoral feeling of Virgil and Giorgione. The elegant lords and ladies whom we see in his pictures sitting together talking or making music in a park, or standing idly by a pool, or wandering over grassy slopes to embark for Cythera, are transfigured by the painter into something greater than they know. Here again, at the full blossoming of an elaborately civilised age, life pauses to reflect upon its achievement, and, attaining consciousness in the artist's mind, reveals to us by the magic of colour the beauty and significance of things in the gathering together of a few people for a simple act of amusement.

Ay, in the very temple of delight
   Veiled melancholy has her sovran shrine
Though seen of none save him whose strenuous tongue
   Can burst Joy's grape against his palate fine ;
His soul shall taste the sadness of her might,
   And be among her cloudy trophies hung.

THE
CONSOLATIONS OF CICERO

→►◆◄←

In his eloquent and sweeping condemnation of Cicero's character, career, and literary achievements, Mommsen does not spare the Correspondence : ' People are in the habit of calling it interesting and clever; and it is so, as long as it reflects the urban or villa life of the world of quality ; but where the writer is thrown on his own resources, as in exile, in Cilicia and after the battle of Pharsalus, it is stale and empty as was ever the soul of a feuilletonist banished from his familiar circles.' This criticism, while it calls attention to a fundamental weakness in Cicero's character, does not really touch the genius and attraction of the letters ; like much of Mommsen's criticism, it is too ready to condemn the whole for the blemishes of the part, to appreciate every character entirely by the rightness or wrongness of its political sense. It is, indeed, only through the letters that we come to know this particular weakness of Cicero, but their true interest is spread everywhere over their surface, revealing all sides of a personality in perfect intimacy. It is not really the description of urban or villa life which constitutes the charm of the letters, except for those whose chief joy lies in the formal reconstruction of ancient life ;

their charm is an essentially living one—the contact with the mind and personality of a very gifted man who lived through one of the great epochs of history.

Interesting and important, where they still survive, for all periods of his life and for the general history of the times, the letters become most engrossing with the beginning of the Civil War. During the first half of 49 B.C. Cicero wrote almost daily to Atticus, and we can follow in the most minute fashion every thought and emotion that passes across the surface of his mind. The politician and historian may be contemptuous of this perpetual weighing of reasons, this delicate balance between personal and public feeling, this continual shelving of responsibilities. But the reader who has the gift of sympathetic imagination, and can be touched by the failures as well as by the greatness of human nature, can enter into contact through these letters with the actual mind, freed from all the trappings of literary or public convention, of a man who, though he may have had little appreciable effect on the political history of Rome, has been one of the greatest forces in the civilisation and culture of Western Europe.

As long as a man is held by the routine of work in the pursuit of his ambition or in the winning of his daily bread, the strength of his will and the resources of his character may be known neither to himself nor to others. The meaning of life in general as opposed to this or that contingent

THE CONSOLATIONS OF CICERO

activity has never been considered. Then by some unexpected chance he is forced to retire for a time from the world of affairs and is suddenly brought face to face with the simple reality of himself:

> At last
> The language of sincerity and truth
> Is wrung forth from the bottom of his heart :
> The mask is torn off ; what is real remains.[1]

The great poet from whom those lines are translated died in 55 B.C., and the brief notice of Cicero about the work of Lucretius was written to his brother in 54 B.C., when the orator's political activities were more or less dependent upon the will of the triumvirs. But this passage, and much else in the poem, can hardly have failed to bring back vividly to his thoughts the weary months of his exile in 58-57 B.C., when, cut off for the first time in his career from public life, he was forced to examine his scale of values. The searching analysis to which Lucretius subjects the ambitions of public life may well be responsible in part for the silence in which Cicero passes over the poem except for this brief and inadequate criticism. Much of it must have seemed a penetrating and unwelcome diagnosis of his own spiritual experience :

> He read each wound, each weakness clear,
> And struck his finger on the place
> And said—*Thou ailest here and here.*[2]

---

[1] Lucretius, III. 57, trans. R. C. Trevelyan.
[2] Matthew Arnold, *Memorial Verses*.

Yet we must in justice admit that Cicero had some ground for complaint at his exile, though not to such an extent as he indulged in, if we realise the full significance to him of that blow. He was not yet fifty years old, and according to the standard of Roman public life he was still a young man ; he shone brightly, to himself at least, as a star of the first magnitude in the heaven of politics. As a statesman and lawyer his time was so occupied that, in spite of his culture, he never seems to have thought that anything more than success in daily business was necessary for the happiness of life. And then in exile he discovered that all the expectations of a great consular and of an eloquent counsel had been suddenly annihilated by the vindictiveness of a worthless demagogue and the indifference of men whom he had imagined to be his friends and supporters.

Exceptional as Cicero's gifts and culture were, he was yet a true and typical Roman in his complete identification of himself with the life of the State and of the city of Rome. In this respect he was worthy of an earlier and better generation. In one of the letters, written to Atticus at the outbreak of the Civil War, he says : ' My opinion was that our city and people must be established for immortality so far as in us lay.' And this immortality of Rome he opposes to the essential mortality of the individual. The life of the city and of the State was for Cicero the sole reality

THE CONSOLATIONS OF CICERO

from which the rest of life received its value. It was bound up inseparably with the reality of the true Roman gods—or rather, the gods' existence was bound up with that of the State. Such, at least, is the inference we are justified in drawing from the expressions of Cicero and Varro, a much more profound and learned antiquarian. Commenting on Varro's statement that he had written of human antiquities before treating of the divine ones, because the divine ones had been founded by men, Warde Fowler writes:

> This no doubt refers rather to the various cults, which had in fact been instituted by the State; but it implies, in characteristic Roman fashion, that the gods would have been nothing to the Romans if the State had not established their worship. Nay, he can go a step further and say that the very existence of the gods depends on that worship—a view in one sense profoundly true at Rome, as elsewhere in the pagan world. In another passage he expresses a fear lest some of them should perish simply from neglect.[1]

Unless we realise this intimate relationship between State and deity, so that the one is little less than the visible form of the other, constituting the sole reality for the individual, we cannot sympathetically understand Cicero's interminable vacillation at the outbreak of war in 49 B.C. He could not bring himself to do anything that might

[1] Warde Fowler, *Roman Ideas of Deity*, p. 82.

THE CONSOLATIONS OF CICERO

accelerate the destruction of the State, for with its destruction was implied the withdrawal of the divine element from the world of his experience. The solid ground of the Roman State was crumbling beneath his feet, or, as Atticus wrote to him, 'The sun seems to have set for ever.'

Yet it is at this period of his life that we are justified in demanding more resistance and resource from Cicero. He was nearly sixty. The last ten years of his life had been rich in deceptions, disappointments, and adversity. For many years his political activities had been regulated by the wishes of Cæsar and Pompey. He can hardly have concealed from himself the fact that he had little more to expect in public life. He himself admits that age was making itself felt, and his terrible uncertainty of plan during the first half of 49 B.C. may have been to some extent due to a failure of nerve, showing itself in a disinclination to the hardships of travelling and campaigning. For some time after the battle of Pharsalus he was in considerable doubt whether the Pompeians might not finally defeat Cæsar, and this thought filled him with fear for his own life as well as with remorse for having failed to support with more vigour the cause which he had finally adopted of his own free will. Indeed the eleven months which Cicero spent at Brundisium, from October 48 B.C. to September in the next year, are the most desolate and distressing part of his life.

THE CONSOLATIONS OF CICERO

For this sojourn at Brundisium reveals definitely to us that Cicero, now an old man and faced with uncertainty, possible exile or death, had no inner life at all. He had not in his composition a grain of that stoicism which many Romans possessed. His vivid imagination and sensitiveness took complete control of his mind. He did not even feel that his conscience was clear, and realised too late that adherence to theory means little unless there is some final bar at which that adherence can be justified. He confesses openly to Atticus that he has sinned in his policy; that no one else has put himself in the same plight, open to the charge of being lukewarm to both sides. He doubts his own integrity, and looks everywhere to find some one to approve his policy. Nor is it only fear about the fate of his country which causes Cicero's unhappiness. There is little mention of the State in the letters of these months. He knew that, whichever party won, the Republic was doomed. The fear was for his own future, whether he would be allowed to spend his remaining years in Rome or have to endure exile again or even death. He feared most of all the victory of the Pompeians, whom he once thought to be the upholders of the constitution. Of literature or philosophy there is not a word; no mention of any consolation to be derived from immersion in the experience of others; no effort to create anything himself; the arts of which he had talked so bravely were an

THE CONSOLATIONS OF CICERO

ornament of social culture and in no way a reality of the inner life. Human relationships were not more effectual. He welcomes Atticus's letters because they afford a momentary relief during the act of reading. His estrangement from his wife Terentia became complete; and, worst of all, even the arrival of his dearly-loved daughter Tullia brought no consolation to him; it rather increased his misery by the consciousness of the sorrow which she suffered through his own fault. There is no trace of comfort coming to him through their mutual affection and sympathy. He is surprised, and even a little exasperated, by the equanimity with which Tullia bears her own afflictions, the faithlessness and unkindness of her husband Dolabella. He cannot understand her self-control. 'I have never seen anything like her,' he writes to Atticus; and in another letter, summing up briefly the hopeless prospect of his position inwardly and externally : 'No consolation can afford me the slightest relief. My sufferings are not due to chance—then they would be endurable—but I have brought everything upon myself by my own bodily and mental mistakes and weakness.' There at last is the truth from his own lips, the recognition of his foolishness and guilt, the bitter and involuntary confession in old age that he had learned nothing from the experiences of life, but had fallen helplessly between the demands of fact and theory.

THE CONSOLATIONS OF CICERO

Some time during the year 46—most probably in the second half of it—Cicero, comfortably re-established in Rome, without official relations with Cæsar but in touch with his supporters, wrote a number of letters to various friends and acquaintances who, not yet reconciled with the new master of Rome, were living in exile in various parts of the Empire. Among them was the consular M. Claudius Marcellus and such prominent men as Aulus Torquatus, the learned Pythagorean Publius Figulus, Ligarius and Plancius, representing in varying degree the types of Roman character. Some of them were well known to Cicero ; with others the letter of condolence was no more than a matter of form, yet there is little variation either in style or tone. They are all of them carefully-considered expressions of opinion, putting forward various reasons for comfort and confidence with which a Roman might fortify himself amid the ruins of the free republican State. It is unlikely that Cicero would have written in them anything which he knew would either hurt the susceptibilities or contradict the accepted conventions of his correspondents. We are justified, then, in assuming that they give us very fair material for estimating the outlook on life of the upper-class Roman in his private capacity during the last years of the Republic. And, coming in such close juxtaposition to that dark period of Cicero's despair at Brundisium before he was

THE CONSOLATIONS OF CICERO

forgiven by Cæsar, they throw much illumination on the curious mentality of the orator, his speedy forgetfulness of the past, his complete subjection to the narcotic of fine language and thought—almost a case of self-hypnotism—his inability to suggest anything which would really bring consolation to an empty life. And this inability is not due to the weakness of Cicero's mind, but to the prevailing conditions of culture and thought of the world in which he lived. In these letters judgment is passed unconsciously upon the age by one who represented some of its best qualities. How empty and powerless to console would Cicero have found one of these letters could he have received it during the year 48-47 B.C. at Brundisium.

The bitterness of exile from Rome—such is the general tenor of these stately letters—is much mitigated by the knowledge that the constitution is dead and free political life at an end. It is better to avoid the sight of such a catastrophe by absence. There is also much consolation to be derived from the possession of a good conscience—that is, from the knowledge of having had a right will in the past—of having fought on the constitutional side, even though the prospect, should that party have conquered, would have been extremely gloomy. Cicero seems to have entirely forgotten his frequent cries of 'Peccavi' to Atticus, when he now claims for himself as well as for those who had actually fought this mode of consolation.

THE CONSOLATIONS OF CICERO

He would have them draw, as he himself does, a melancholy consolation from the fact that they foresaw the actual course of events and were more intelligent than others. And if these considerations are insufficient, as they might well be, if the weight of misery caused by the ruin of all hopes of future activity in the public service is overwhelming, there is the assurance that one day death will bring oblivion of everything. What Servius Sulpicius puts forward as a possibility in his famous letter to Cicero, that the dead might have consciousness, Cicero in several places emphatically denies. 'Death,' he says, 'brings with it freedom from all consciousness, so that we ought to pray for it. One event awaits us all which will bring with it the end of all grief.'

Such consolations are indeed of a very negative and desolating character. The only positive contribution Cicero has to make is the refuge of literature, and this he offers to several of his correspondents, though he himself, in a similar position, had been totally unable to employ it. But when installed once more in his house at Rome or in a villa, he can write with his curious power of self-delusion to the great scholar Varro about the collapse of public life, and say that this only affects those who, unlike himself, have not provided themselves with some resource against the changes and chances of life. 'Your days of study at Tusculum I count as the equal of a whole life, and I would

THE CONSOLATIONS OF CICERO

willingly concede to others all the riches of the world, if only I could live thus free from all interruption. And indeed we do imitate such a life, as far as is possible, and find repose in study.' And again in a letter to the exile Ampius Balbus, a vigorous supporter of Pompey, he writes : ' Literature is our only refuge, which we have always used. In prosperity it was our delight and now it is our salvation.' This consideration of literature is the only one founded on individual characteristics ; the rest are general and show how starved and shallow was the inner life of the average Roman, how dependent on external and uncontrollable interests to give it any continuous meaning. In the following year, replying to a letter of condolence from an old friend Lucceius, he recognises at last the necessity of a deeper inner life for true happiness. ' I consider it the great merit of the philosopher to be independent of external support and to have the reasons of happiness and unhappiness contained in himself.' But the exiles to whom Cicero was writing were very far from this position, and the consoler is really as helpless as the consoled, falling back finally upon such natural strength of mind as they may possess and rehearsing to them the great commonplaces of mortality.

A few months after these letters had been written, Cicero was himself in bitter need of consolation. Very few letters survive from the end of 46 and the beginning of 45 B.C. He was busy watching over the life of his daughter Tullia. Her health had been weak for some time, and she never rallied after the birth of a son in January, and died about the middle of February in her father's villa at Tusculum. Cicero was in despair. He spent the first weeks of his sorrow in Atticus's house in Rome, and then at the beginning of March retired to a lonely villa situated on the delta of the River Astura, on the coast of Latium, southeast of Antium. 'The loneliness of the place,' he writes to Atticus, 'is less painful than the society of Rome.' While staying with Atticus, he had read in very characteristic manner everything that had been written about the abatement of sorrow. He now started to write a Consolation for himself. This he found more helpful than reading, which only distracted his thoughts and did not mitigate the passion of his grief. He found comfort, too, in solitude. Each morning he used to wander away into the dense woods which surrounded the villa and remain there until evening. And then there recurs to him an idea, which he had already discussed with Atticus in the first weeks of his sorrow, that he must do something to perpetuate the memory of Tullia, to raise her above the lot of ordinary mortals, to bring her spirit back to earth as a presence which he and all future generations may respect and venerate. ' I will consecrate her with all the means possible in these learned times, with every kind of memorial known to the genius of Greeks and Romans.' He will build a small shrine (*fanum*) for her, which shall remain inviolate for all time. 'The thought of all the long time to come after my death moves me far more than the few years of life, though they are too long, that are still left to me.' By these strange words he appears to mean that he will somehow or other secure her immortality, however much the carrying out of the plan for the shrine may keep opening the wound of his affliction. And then in letter after letter Cicero slowly unfolds and elaborates his plan. He wished to buy a small garden property on which he could erect the shrine—he makes it very clear that the building is in no way to be thought of as a tomb—and secure her deification ; perhaps canonisation would better represent his Greek word *apotheosis*. The beautiful situation of Astura at first commended itself to him. But he did not see how to secure the perpetual sanctity of the shrine in the changes of ownership which must occur some time in the future. He would prefer it to be near Rome, beside a highroad, or in some frequented locality where passers-by would see it and do reverence to Tullia's spirit, just as the chorus in the *Alkestis* say that the heroine's tomb shall not be considered a tomb but the dwelling-place of a blessed spirit which travellers will greet as they pass on their way. Indeed, the idea of this canonisation of

THE CONSOLATIONS OF CICERO

Tullia very probably came to Cicero from contemporary Greek religious usage, where heroisation of a departed member of a family by the survivors was quite common, giving a higher and stronger existence after death, by which they are distinguished from the mass of the departed.

' I want a frequented spot for the shrine '—*celebritatem sequor*—is the expression which Cicero employs several times in these letters, as though he felt, in accordance with the ordinary Roman conception of the divine, that the immortality of Tullia's spirit depended to some extent on recognition by the living. He is willing to devote all his available capital and to live in the quietest manner possible if he can only secure perpetual ownership of a small plot of land. 'I dread changes of ownership.' First one and then another site comes up for discussion, and each one has its attendant difficulties of purchase and possession, involving long negotiation. In this way month succeeds month, and, in spite of Cicero's protest that he would feel himself a guilty sinner if the whole business was not finished during the summer of 45, the plan gradually fades away, and after a letter of July 26 we have no further mention either of sites or shrine. It seems not unlikely that Cicero finally abandoned the project which he had formed in the first agony of his grief. The passage of time may have lessened his assurance that Tullia's spirit must survive the death of

THE CONSOLATIONS OF CICERO

her body. Pecuniary difficulties may also have stood in the way, and the great cycle of ethical and theological writings on which Cicero started during this year, originating primarily in her death and carried on from the absence of any other interest, may have gradually absorbed his emotional overflow and induced in him for the time being a more philosophic standpoint.

Mr. Warde Fowler, in his book on *The Religious Experience of the Roman People*, claims that ' Cicero, always impressionable and in his way religious, had in this year 45 a real religious experience. He was brought face to face with one of the mysterious facts of life and with one of the great mysteries of the universe, and the religious instinct awoke within him.' Cicero's language and the parallel practice of heroisation in Greek religious usage with which he was familiar from books make such an interpretation rather unnatural. More than once he speaks of this ' consecration ' of Tullia as a vow and a duty which he must perform, as though it were a tribute due to the wonderful virtues of the departed one and a testimony in the eyes of all men ; for that is what is implied in his demand for the publicity and perpetuity of the shrine. He seems to draw more consolation from the fulfilment of this vow than from any thought of the nearness of her immortal spirit and of the possibility of any spiritual relationship. The intense anguish which her death aroused in Cicero

THE CONSOLATIONS OF CICERO

is no doubt largely due to his affection for her, but some of it arises from the fact that by her death the last external reality of his life was swept away. As he writes in reply to Servius Sulpicius's letter of condolence, he had been able to find comfort and repose with Tullia amid the disasters of the State, but now that she was dead he had nowhere to turn for refuge or consolation. Once more his life had lost its centre of gravity, and it would seem that Cicero's immersion in philosophic work during the rest of the year does represent a definite desire to base life upon inner reality rather than on external things. How far his inner life was strengthened by this work we are not in a position to say. The last months of his life, when he was again in the clutches of adversity, remain a blank. But the gift of easy and dignified exposition made translation from the Greek flow so swiftly that any real deepening of his consciousness from a searching analysis of the problems of religious and philosophic thought seems excluded.

Cicero's experience on Tullia's death is a unique and absorbing episode, not only for the insight it gives into his mode of thought and emotion, but because it shows that the need of a more personal religion with some definite spiritual conviction and hope of immortality was making itself felt amid the desolate materialism of a decaying formalism. The letters of this period, combined with those written at Brundisium and the consolatory letters of 46 B.C., give a very clear picture of the insufficiency of the current ideals of life and of the need of something more solid and more sustaining. Cicero was above the level of his age in more ways than in literary and rhetorical skill. He possessed that natural integrity of character which had been the general characteristic of an earlier and happier age. He set his face absolutely against the Epicureanism which had become so popular at Rome ; his antipathy to that way of life may have obscured for him the greatness of Lucretius's genius. 'Such things,' he writes after a gay dinner party during the Cæsarian régime, 'did not appeal to me when young, much less now that I am old.' On the other hand, he had none of the natural stoicism and solid commonsense of the average Roman. His intellectual training and culture were wider and deeper than that of most of his contemporaries. But there can be no doubt that he came to literature through his oratorical gifts. He read widely both in Greek and Latin literature to enrich his own powers of expression, to enlarge the means of his appeal. It is very improbable that the poets of Italy or the great tragedians and philosophers and orators of Greece were a real influence in his life. He has many charming pages on the pleasures of literature ; graceful tributes to the great artists of Greece—elegant expositions of all that literature may be in life ; but there is no glow of emotion

THE CONSOLATIONS OF CICERO

in his words, and in times of difficulty it obviously meant nothing to him. He had not the true *amor intellectualis Dei* of Spinoza's vision. And if literature was of no avail in times of distress, the union of family life was equally found wanting. The worries and doubts by which Cicero was oppressed after the battle of Pharsalus produced estrangement and finally divorce from Terentia, to whom he had been married for thirty years. The affection of his daughter, which he returned too in his own way, brought no relief from the endless toil of his thoughts, and it is not unlikely that a feeling of not having made the most of her sympathy may have rendered more acute his sorrow on her death. Religion, as men knew it in Rome, whether in the worship of the State or the family, had no message for the individual, and with the ruin of the State the security of religion too, such as it was, was shaken.

'The Cicero whom the world reveres,' writes Professor Conway, ' is the man he grew to be in the last decade of his life. In the great years of the Civil War he learned and unlearned much. The childish things that disfigured his earlier days have at last been put away.' [1] Perhaps ' revere ' is too strong a word to use of our feelings towards any one whose humanity, with all its weaknesses, is so well known to us. Even his style, wonderful as it is, is too even in all its occasions, too unvisited

[1] *New Studies of a Great Inheritance*, p. 15.

by glimpses of real emotion, to move us reverentially. We revere the intense earnestness and the passionate vision of Lucretius ; he is a master and a teacher, aloof and serene, with whom we could never be familiar. There is much to respect in Cicero at all periods of his life, but his faults and failings remained with him to the end, redeemed by the persistence of his isolated patriotism. It was the necessity of the times rather than the wisdom of experience which finally put aside for him the childish things of his earlier days. At the end of his life he became a pathetic, almost a tragic figure, in the hopelessness both of his inaction and of his action ; pathetic most of all in his vain effort to find something permanent to which he might cling in a world that was as shifting as sand. The treatises of those years, whose dignified and edifying sentiment contrasts so strangely with the monotonous moral indifference of the world to whom they were offered, are a witness for himself, at least, that the time was ripe for some new gospel of life to re-create society, not from the outside by the will and law of the State, but from within, working outwards to vitalise the whole through the individual.

THE
LANDSCAPE OF VIRGIL

THE idea of Italian scenery as it exists in the English mind is principally formed from the paintings of the old masters and of our own Turner, filled out in some cases by a few recollections of Virgil or the famous poem of Goethe, in which, as Heine says, he has expressed for northerners the whole spirit of Italy. From illustrated Bibles and prints of Italian paintings we have learned to imagine delicate trees, clear skies, large spaces and backgrounds of distant hills as forming the essence of southern scenery, while, before the beginning of the nineteenth century, Goethe expressed in romantic form the vision of statue and marble palace, of cypress and orange trees stirred by a gentle breeze beneath a blue sky. And yet the reality is very different from that ideal scenery. Goethe has taken all the scattered elements of romantic beauty and moulded them by the music of his verse into an unforgettable vision of the promised land. The actual traveller finds them all separated ; orange and lemon trees [1] grow chiefly along the Riviera coast and in the south ; olive groves are rare on the north side of the Apennines ; the marble palace is

[1] Introduced into Italy during the Crusades.

THE LANDSCAPE OF VIRGIL

closed and only its façade is visible from a narrow street; the statue is unfeelingly exposed to the public gaze in a museum. But the magical spell created in our minds by history and the art of the past still abides with us in an altered but equally romantic form, predisposing us to find beauty everywhere. And that indefinable Italian atmosphere, which is the counterpart in reality of the poet's verse and the painter's colour, is always there to charm away the hours of slow travelling by the grace with which it invests a landscape, possessing in its own forms the simplicity and harmony of a work of art.

Among the great lovers and singers of Italy, Virgil will always hold the place of honour :

> Hither as to their fountain other stars
> Repairing, in their golden urns draw light,
> And hence the morning planet gilds his horns.

And yet that part of his work which deals most intimately with Italian scenery is the most difficult for his readers to appreciate. There are few who enjoy the *Georgics* in later life without having first learned to love Italy by visiting the country and becoming penetrated with her spirit through knowledge of her art and observation of the varieties of her landscape. Interest is often blunted by the difficulties of vocabulary, by our own ignorance of agricultural life, and by the consciousness that his treatment is disconnected and

THE LANDSCAPE OF VIRGIL

his practical advice long since superseded. We are finally contented to remember the *Georgics* only by the large 'purple patches,' which emphasise superficially the unevenness of the work and by their rather artificial brilliance prevent us from seeing the deeper revelation of the poet's mind in his interpretation of the ordinary life of the farmer. The forces of nature, morning and evening, light and darkness, the gifts and refusals of the earth, are the same now as in Virgil's time. They are the permanent 'setting' for our life, and by showing them to us under the light of his own imagination Virgil fulfils in Shelley's language the function of the poet, for if we listen to him carefully he purges 'from our inward sight the film of familiarity which obscures from us the wonder of our being.'

Virgil was a lover of the country as well as a 'landscape lover,' to use Tennyson's phrase, and it is the combination of these two quite distinct qualities that gives the *Georgics* their peculiar fascination. His gift for describing idyllic scenery or historic sites is conspicuous in the *Eclogues* and *Æneid*; in the *Georgics* that gift is consecrated to more significant purposes. It is not actual or ideal scenery that Virgil describes in these poems, but the processes of nature, and above all else the process of life as men carry it on, sometimes apparently in conflict with nature, at other times with her help. The landscape is never out of relation to man. It is little more than a background, shown in the briefest manner, and strictly relevant to the action of the subject, yet always suggesting, like the backgrounds in the work of the Central Italian painters, the infinite space in which the incidents of life occur, the overhanging sky, the intense heat of summer, the sweep of clouds or wind over the fields, the serenity of cloudless evenings, the influences of sunlight and moonlight.

The greater part of the *Georgics* is occupied with discussions about the nature of certain animals, trees and crops, on which the farmer's prosperity depends, and with those simple processes of agriculture which we have watched again and again with varying degrees of interest. At first sight it is not an easy poetical theme, and, as though he were conscious of this difficulty, Virgil has not hesitated to let himself be drawn into digressions. These digressions are the ' purple passages ' of the *Georgics*, in which the superficial reader may find the chief beauty of the poem. Beauty, indeed, they most certainly have, but it is the beauty of an untroubled Eden, of an idyllic Arcadian life forgetful of the burden of the world. The passages describing the glory and fertility of Italy, the blessings of the farmer's life, the Tarentine garden, appear slightly unreal when read with the main body of a work which is so occupied with the simple and eternal things of the earth and man's tragic struggle for existence. Even those shorter passages of only a

THE LANDSCAPE OF VIRGIL

few lines with which Virgil variegates and seeks to relieve the severity of his theme, though they may have been welcome to the citizen of Rome, seem rhetorical to an age that looks on nature with a direct gaze. The saffron of Tmolus, the ivory of India, the incense of Sabæa, sound remote and artificial in our ears beside the fields of beans with rattling pods, the crops of slender vetch, the brittle stalks and rustling undergrowth of the 'sour lupin.' We prefer to see the strong oxen turning up the rich soil, to feel the full heat of the midsummer sun baking the clods into dust, conscious that such things are the enduring substance of life surviving all temporary modifications or extravagances. And this consciousness of the importance and permanence of these simple things comes to us not from any explicit reference, but principally by means of the dignity of Virgil's hexameters. There is everywhere implicit in the *Georgics* that spirit to which Thomas Hardy has given full expression in his poem *The Breaking of Nations* :

> Only a man harrowing clods,
> In a slow silent walk,
> With an old horse that stumbles and nods,
> Half asleep as they stalk.
>
> Only thin smoke without flame
> From the heaps of couch grass :
> Yet this will go onward the same
> Though Dynasties pass.

Yonder a maid and her wight
Come whispering by :
War's annals will cloud into night
Ere their story die.

And the solemn utterance of his verse is assisted by another gift, the peculiar possession of great poets, that power of 'synoptic vision,' which Plato considers to be the distinguishing mark of the philosophic mind. Though Virgil's eye may be turned for the moment upon some particular need of soil, or seed, or tree, practical details are always pervaded by the other influences of nature. The sun and moon, the stars, and the air of heaven give the occasions for ploughing and sowing and reaping. The south-west wind has its secret purpose ; the soil is sensitive to heat and frost, and man himself does not understand all the secret forces that work in it.[1] The poor bean and Egyptian lentil depend upon the setting of Boötes. Lucerne and millet must be thought of when the 'sun with Taurus rides.' The vine, the giver of joy and life, must not face towards the setting sun.

An admirable instance of Virgil's power to infuse into the single occurrence the greatness of the whole and to unite all things together in poetic vision is the passage about spring in the second *Georgic*. The idea of spring, even in Virgil's time, had become a somewhat hackneyed theme for poets ; yet even in the most conven-

[1] *Georgics*, i. 89. *Cæca spiramenta*.

tional part of his description he touches our sensibilities anew by his delicate attribution of human feeling to the swelling seeds and buds, and by the fine image of the fields baring their bosoms to the wooing of the mild west wind :

> Zephyrique tepentibus auris
> Laxant arva sinus.

> The fields
> Unlock their bosoms to the warm west winds.[1]

But this picture of spring's annual beauty is quickly lost in the sublime imagination of that great creative spring, when ' God first dawned on Chaos ' and the earth for the first time was clothed with grass and flowers. The few lines that describe this vision have all the vastness and majesty of Milton's inspiration, and at the close achieve a sublime brevity that Milton never accomplished, throwing the creation of the first three days into one line :

> Inmissæque feræ silvis et sidera cœlo.

> And wild beasts thronged the woods, and stars the heaven.

By this sudden reference to its mysterious beginning the wonder of the earth here and now is brought close to us, and we are sharply awoken to the deeper significance of each ' revolving spring,' when the hardness of existence is for a

[1] The translations are from the version by James Rhoades.

brief space mitigated, and the spirit of life has a chance to develop. For here, too, as in many other places in Virgil and in his predecessor Lucretius, the pathos of existence, as an unequal struggle in a world whose vital forces are failing, is revealed. We become, strangely enough, most conscious of the fragility of human things, of the uncertainty of the earth's assistance, by this aspect of spring as the moment when the plants and seeds, upon which man's life depends, have a brief remission from their struggle for existence and can grow in confidence. Man must increase his efforts to assist the failing power of the earth, so as to produce that from which her children live.

> These have I seen degenerate, did not man
> Put forth his hand with power, and year by year
> Choose out the largest. So, by fate impelled,
> Speed all things to the worse and backward borne
> Glide from us.[1]

This life of toil, though, ideally, man imagines his happiness to rest in remission from it, is really that in which such happiness as is possible for him is to be won. He must learn to wait upon the seasons, to acquiesce in the wider laws of the natural world. If at any moment he pauses, thinking he has achieved a happiness that can be enjoyed apart from the process of life, the imagined treasure dissolves into thin air within his arms.

[1] *Georgics*, i. 197.

THE LANDSCAPE OF VIRGIL

His fate is symbolised in the parting of Eurydice and Orpheus :

Immemor heu ! victusque animi respexit ; ibi omnis
Effusus labor.
                      But even with the look,
Poured out was all his labour, broken the bond
Of that fell tyrant . . .

Everywhere in the *Georgics*, except in the digressions, the Italian country is for Virgil the scene of labour. The nobler animals, the horse and the ox, seem consciously to assist man, and in one place, at least, Virgil remonstrates with the earth —*iustissima tellus*—for showing no consideration of their simple and toilsome lives. This presumed sensibility gives a wonderful pathos to those lines in which he meditates on the death of the ploughing ox :

                      What now
Besteads him toil or service ? To have turned
The heavy sod with ploughshare ? And yet these
Ne'er knew the Massic wine-god's baneful boon,
Nor twice replenished banquets : but on leaves
They fare, and virgin grasses, and their cups
The crystal springs and streams with running tired,
Their healthful slumbers never broke by care.[1]

---
[1] *Georgics*, iii. 525.
  Quid labor aut benefacta iuvant ? quid vomere terras
  Invertisse graves ? atqui non Massica Bacchi
  Munera, non illis epulæ nocuere repostæ. . . .
  Frondibus et victu pascuntur simplicis herbæ,
  Pocula sunt fontes liquidi atque exercita cursu
  Flumina, nec somnos abrumpit cura salubris.

THE LANDSCAPE OF VIRGIL

Exercita cursu flumina ; the very streams share in the labours of man and beast.

It is as a setting for the life of toil that we become familiar with the various aspects of the landscape which Virgil loved. The countryside of the *Georgics* is not exclusively taken from the Lombardy plain, and the view is gaining ground that Virgil freely mingled features from the life of South Italy both in the *Georgics* and the *Eclogues*. When he is writing most intimately of the country he becomes most universal and timeless, dwelling on details which seem common to all lands. Of course he can also describe the distinctive features of the southern landscape, but through the greater part of the *Georgics* we feel that his countryside, like the backgrounds in Perugino's or Raphael's pictures, is almost northern in its subdued and tranquil beauty. In the course of the farmer's year we learn to feel the full significance of many aspects of nature, which we can all appreciate ; the shortening days and mellow heat of autumn : the chill rain and driven clouds of late autumn ; the snow and ice of winter, when the farmer is kept indoors and lamps are lit early ; the appearance of heavy storm clouds ; the sea birds blown inland before rough weather ; the forests bending beneath the north wind ; the varying brightness of the moon and stars ; the sodden wretchedness of the fields after great rain ; the last leaves fluttering to the

THE LANDSCAPE OF VIRGIL

ground in the wood or vineyard after an autumn frost.

And within these larger and universal forms of landscape he places those brief descriptions, often only a line or two, in which recollection and reality are woven together into the perfect harmony of rhythmical utterance. This gift of the 'lonely word' or line is the quality which has made Virgil peculiarly dear to lovers of Italy, who find in him the ideal interpreter of scenery, which has a definite spiritual quality for their eyes. The real felicity of such lines can be realised best by those who have enjoyed in a detached mood the scenes that he evokes. The lines seem to carry in themselves not only the fullness of actual life, but something more, a mysterious over-value, too deep for words, by means of which this single incident possesses the whole joy and burden of life. Who that has once seen in Italy the oxen slowly dragging the plough through the spaces between the rows of vines can fail to recognise the perfect adequacy of his line :

> Flectere luctantes inter vineta iuvencos,
>
> Ply up and down
> Your labouring bullocks through the vineyard's midst,

while at the same time the rhythm and alliteration raise it far above the plane of simple description. And the same thing takes place in that other

THE LANDSCAPE OF VIRGIL

picture of the harvesting, when the laden wagons roll slowly homewards from the fields :

> Nulloque ex æquore cernes
> Plura domum tardis decedere plaustra iuvencis,

> From no field
> More wains thou 'lt see wend home with plodding steers,

and the season of the vintage when :

> Mitis in apricis coquitur vindemia saxis,

> On sunny rocks the mellowing vintage bakes,

where in each case the sound of the line carries us out from the particular occasion into the serenity of artistic experience. And who has ever expressed more perfectly the slow progress of a day of perfect weather among the flocks in summer : the coolness of dawn, the cropping of the grass, the gathering heat, the delight of deep shadow ; and at sunset the freshening influence of the dew, the rising of the moon, and the evening song of the birds heard where the cliffs break down to the sea ? [1]

Virgil's variety is infinite,[2] and even in his feeling towards landscape we must distinguish different modes of self-expression. Most apparent in the *Georgics* is that serious and significant inter-

---

[1] *Georgics*, iii. 322. The same feeling pervades Giorgione's 'Fête Champêtre.'

[2] Cf., for instance, the romantic solemnity of the scene A. i. 162 *seq.* with the low tones and luminous space of A. vii. 30 *seq.*

THE LANDSCAPE OF VIRGIL

pretation of the earth, not only as the scene of man's effort, but as an element of that life, inseparably connected with his misery or happiness. The earth is a necessary part in the design of life. In the *Eclogues*, on the other hand, and in one famous passage in the second *Georgic*—the eulogy of the farmer's life—Virgil strikes the frankly idyllic and artificial note of Arcadian existence. In these places we feel that he is describing a country life not as it actually is, but as it might appeal to the imagination of a tired and confined city dweller. The toil and anxiety and disappointment of the farmer are hidden from view, and he is seen in the midst of a happy family, in fair summer weather, enjoying the fruits of his land, while in the *Eclogues* the loveliness of nature and the delight of spring weather beside clear streams is the setting for the lover's suit. His models in this manner of writing were the Greek Bucolic poets, but the Roman language even in Virgil's hands was incapable of reproducing the lightness and swiftness of the Greek thought and rhythm, which makes us pass over the artificiality of much of Theocritus's best work in virtue of the complete harmony of form and content. The heavier cadence of the Latin hexameter could never maintain the buoyancy and varied grace of the famous 'Harvesting' in Cos,[1] which may almost disguise for us the fact that it is, after all,

[1] Theocritus, vii.

THE LANDSCAPE OF VIRGIL

an experience of townsmen, to whom the real joy and significance of the country are denied. The deeper emotion of the *Georgics* is far beyond the compass of Theocritus's nature, while Virgil does not convince us of the careless happiness of his Arcadia. The landscape in which he places the shepherds of the *Eclogues* is charming and idyllic ; the sun is always shining ; the clear streams murmur gently between green banks ; the cool cave or the fresh grass beneath the poplar invite song or sleep.

> Here glows the Spring, here Earth
> Beside the streams pours forth a thousand flowers ;
> Here the white poplar bends above the cave,
> And the lithe vine weaves shadowy covert : come,
> Leave the mad waves to beat upon the shore.[1]

But there always remains something of the *décor de théâtre* about these scenes. Think, for instance, in the eulogy of the farmer's life (*Georgics*, ii. 458 *seq.*) of the contrast between the idyllic picture of the happy family for whom

> The year o'erflows with fruit,
> Or young of kine, or Ceres' wheaten sheaf,
> With crops the furrow loads, and burst the barns,

---

[1] *Eclogues*, ix. 41.
  Hic ver purpureum, varios hic flumina circum
  Fundit humus flores, hic candida populus antro
  Imminet et lentæ texunt umbracula vites ;
  Huc ades ; insani feriant sine litora fluctus.

Cf. i. 51, 74 ; v. 45 ; x. 42.

and the serious effort of the line with which that description commences:

> Agricola incurvo terram dimovit aratro.
>
> The husbandman
> With hooked, ploughshare turns the soil.

This line is pregnant with the ceaseless struggle against opposing forces, with the dignity of the toiling life so much more real than the ' broad-acred ease '—*latis otia fundis*—of the ' gentleman farmer,' which Virgil dwells on at such length. And the same air of artificiality hangs over his prayer to be transported to

> Spercheius and Taygete,
> By Spartan maids o'er revelled ! Oh, for one
> Would set me in deep dells of Hæmus cool.

For the moment the serious things of life are forgotten and the poet's fancy plays with the thought of a blissful Arcadian existence, though in the depth of his heart—and most of the *Georgics* and *Æneid* bears witness to it—he knew that the highest value of life was to be found in, something very different.

> Redit agricolis labor actus in orbem
> Atque in se sua per vestigia volvitur annus.
>
> Round on the labourer spins the wheel of toil,
> As on its own track rolls the circling year.

And then there are the directly descriptive lines or passages where the poet dwells for a moment on some part of Italy or on some historic spot within the Roman Empire. This is the poetry of reminiscence, effective principally for those who have visited the place or know its nature from literary tradition, and like to have the spirit as well as the predominant physical appearance of the place given to them in precise poetical form.

Arduus inde Acragas ostentat maxima longe
Mœnia magnanimum quondam generator equorum.

Thence towering Acragas displays afar
Her mighty walls, once breeder of braver steeds.

In the southern landscape, which is so devoid of superfluities, a single epithet has a much higher value than in more confused scenery. The visitor to Girgenti who has walked along that line of ruined temples, built on a ridge high above the sea, will not want more local colour than the ' lonely ' adjective *arduus* gives in those two lines. But Virgil knew also that the significance of places for human beings is not exhausted by topographical detail. He weaves into his descriptions a sentiment of the life of places, of the sadness of mortality, pervading not only the magnificence of the past but the strength of the present. He suggests the glory of Girgenti and the splendour of its ruins by the memory of the horses who had often won prizes at the games in Greece for their princely masters :

Magnanimum quondam generator equorum.

THE LANDSCAPE OF VIRGIL

And in the same manner his praise of Italy in the second *Georgic* is appreciated most profoundly by those who know the country. It was only after visiting Lake Garda that Goethe, and Tennyson after him, realised the fullness of Virgil's

> Fluctibus et fremitu assurgens, Benace, marino ;

and how perfectly the memories of hill towns in Umbria or in the valley of the Tiber are enshrined in the two lines :

> Tot congesta manu præruptis oppida saxis,
> Fluminaque antiquos subterlabentia muros.

>   Town on town
> Up rugged precipices heaved and reared
> And rivers undergliding ancient walls,

where the general appearance of such towns is suffused with a spiritual quality drawn from the sound of the verse and from the contrast between the ancient immovable walls and the ceaseless stream of the water, suggesting that permanence in change which makes the mystery of things.

The great catalogue of Italian places in the second half of the seventh *Æneid* shows a patriotic love of his country no less than an appreciation of its landscape. For himself and the Romans of that period the passage must also have been full of pathos, for many of those towns whose beauty and warlike spirit are celebrated had become deserted or fallen from their high estate to be humble villages ; their temples and the

THE LANDSCAPE OF VIRGIL

old-fashioned worship of their gods were no longer maintained. Yet if the works of man have wasted away, the Divine presences, of whom the legends tell, still linger in the countryside ; the fertility of the earth still remains ; the bond of sympathy which exists between a land and its children still subsists as in the old days when

> Te nemus Angitiæ, vitrea te Fucinus unda
> Te liquidi flevere lacus.
>
> Wept for thee
> Angitia's grove, for thee the glassy wave
> Of Fucinus, the crystal pools for thee.

This part of the *Æneid* gives a wider and truer picture of Italy than the panegyric in the second *Georgic* ; it is the Italy that corresponds to the vision of it in the mind of the northern visitor. Mountains and rocky peaks, clear lakes, hills covered with the vine or the olive tree, winding rivers, thick woods, and gorges and upland pastures,

> et Cimini cum monte lacum lucosque Capenas.
>
> The lake
> and hill of Ciminus and Capena's groves.

And just as all the places were sanctified for Virgil by patriotic tradition, so the modern traveller does not simply see the actual scene of the moment. The most prosaic and unhistorical tourist cannot help seeing it through a thin veil of romance, while others, more immersed in the

THE LANDSCAPE OF VIRGIL

art or the history of Rome and Italy, yield themselves willingly to the influences of imagination and nature, and become absorbed in the mysterious significance of the past. And actually for many travellers the enchantment of Italy lies in its power to secure forgetfulness of the present by a landscape in which the past lives on victoriously with the present. The power of the Eternal City is spread over all Italy.

THE IMPERIAL LEGEND IN SUETONIUS

ALL conscientious visitors to Rome sooner or later pay their respects to the famous bronze wolf in the Conservatori Palace on the Capitol. With the 'Boy pulling out a Thorn,' the 'Venus,' the 'Dying Gladiator' and the 'Fawn' it forms the group of four 'show pieces' in the Capitoline Museums upon which the guides direct all the ardour of their artistic vocabulary. Yet it is probable that for many the most interesting and enduring experience of those two museums comes from the rooms in which the busts of the Roman emperors are collected. The Capitoline collection of portraits is the largest and most complete in Rome, but into whatever museum the visitor goes he will find portraits of the Imperial families of the early Empire—in the National Museum, for instance, there is the famous bronze of Tiberius, in the Vatican the statue of Augustus—until he is able to recognise them without a guide-book, welcoming their appearance as something familiar and concrete amid the long vistas of heavy or insipid Roman copies of Greek divinities and heroes. And these portraits of the emperors, apart from their intrinsic human or historical interest, fall naturally into place with the impres-

THE IMPERIAL LEGEND IN SUETONIUS

sions the visitor receives from the picturesque ruins of Imperial Rome.

Imperial Rome, the Rome of the first century A.D., is the dominating influence in Rome for the tourist. St. Peter's and the Vatican cannot compete with the effect produced by the Forum, the Triumphal Arches, the vast ruins of the Palatine, the indestructible mass of the Colosseum, in which all the extravagancies and cruelties of the Roman emperors are summed up. And this Rome is the Rome of the Twelve Cæsars, whose biographies by the chances of fortune is the only work of the voluminous writer C. Suetonius Tranquillus that has come down to us practically complete. And just as the busts of the Cæsars attract and interest the eye of the weary wanderer in Rome, because they are realised as the actual likenesses of the men who once lived in the palaces of the Palatine and watched the butchery in the Colosseum, so the biographies of Suetonius have maintained themselves by their appeal to common humanity, describing not the forms and procedure of the Imperial government, but details from the lives of those men who, decadent or commonplace by nature, were placed by the caprice of fortune in control of all the resources of the Roman Empire.

The date of Suetonius' birth and death are both unknown to us. His boyhood fell in the reign of Domitian (81-96 A.D.), the last of the twelve

THE IMPERIAL LEGEND IN SUETONIUS

emperors. We have a slight sketch of him from the pen of the younger Pliny who, writing to Bæbius Hispanus, says that Suetonius wishes to buy, if the price is not too large, a small estate which a friend of Bæbius is putting up for auction. 'All that my scholar-friend wants,' says Pliny, 'is space enough in which to lift up his head, rest his tired eyes, where he can saunter round the bounds of his estate, tread the same path day by day, count the vines and trees, and take a personal interest in each one of them.' We learn from another letter of Pliny that Suetonius had a legal practice in Rome. Later he became a private secretary to the Emperor Hadrian, and it was while holding this office that he completed and published the Lives of the Twelve Cæsars, dedicating the book to Septicius Clarus, Prefect of Rome from 119-121 A.D. He had to resign his position as secretary in 121 owing to some indiscretion, and we have no information about the rest of his life. Though he started life in the legal profession, as so many Romans did, Suetonius was essentially a student and a compiler of learned books. The historical section of his works, so far as we know them, is small when compared with his immense productivity in antiquarian, anthropological, and grammatical fields. Like the elder Pliny, he was an unwearying reader of books, an indefatigable maker of excerpts, a 'snapper up of unconsidered trifles' in every department of learning. Writing Greek as easily as Latin, he was, in the fashion of his time, a polymath rather than a man of letters, an antiquarian rather than a historian, and no doubt regarded his *Roma* and *Pratum*, which contained at least ten books, as more likely to bring him enduring fame than these short biographies.

The form in which Suetonius cast his material was based on the accepted style of biography, and the precise uniformity of it was no doubt congenial to this compiler of learned hand-books, freeing him from the burden of creating his own form. But he can never have thought that these biographical studies were real contributions to the science of history, though he has often been harshly criticised in modern times for his lack of historical sense, as though he had claimed to be a professional historian. Suetonius knew quite well what historical writing was, and occasionally shows genuine critical power in dealing with conflicting statements of authorities. His real interest lies in writing character studies of the emperors, nor is his treatment and conception of biography as pedantic as a hurried reading of the Lives might suggest. He is undoubtedly alive to development of character, to the influences of heredity and of environment upon the individual, but he has not enough originality of mind to break down the conventional form of biography and allow himself complete freedom in tracing

THE IMPERIAL LEGEND IN SUETONIUS

those influences. There is considerable variation in the length of each biography, but the order of treatment is invariable. First there is a section dealing with the ancestry of the particular emperor, and the facts and legends connected with his birth; this is followed by an account of his life up to the assumption of the purple; his various political and public actions are, except in the case of Augustus, quickly enumerated; the account of his death is circumstantial, and is always the most carefully written part of each biography, forming a fine dramatic conclusion. The largest number of chapters is devoted to the personal characteristics of each emperor; his peculiarities of dress and manner, his likes and dislikes, his virtues and vices, with anecdotes illustrating his character in the clutch of imperial circumstance. Suetonius is chiefly interested in the emperors as men and in watching the effects of exalted position upon their natures. Too often this interest degenerates into the writing of 'personal paragraphs.'

The best part of the work is undoubtedly the lives of the first six emperors, the principate of the Julio-Claudian family, beginning with Julius Cæsar and ending with Nero. In the case of Julius Cæsar we have also a biography of Plutarch, and, while the two writers coincide in much of their material, the treatment of Suetonius is much more effective in arrangement and more

THE IMPERIAL LEGEND IN SUETONIUS

vigorous in style and interpretation. He makes no attempt to explain the military and political schemes of Cæsar, but without him we should not understand the more intimate aspect of his character. He reveals to us Cæsar's magnetism and charm of manner in the private relations of life, that personal element which played a no less important part in his career than the military genius of which we have ample evidence in the public history of the period. He tells us how Cæsar ate bad olive oil unhesitatingly in order to spare his host's feelings; how he punished his baker for giving his guests an inferior kind of bread to what he received himself; how he slept in the open so that a sick friend might enjoy the only spare bed in a wayside inn. He records the words he addressed to his troops in Africa when they were dismayed at the report of Juba's great forces, words which show his humour and originality in dealing with his troops. 'Let me tell you,' he said, 'that in a few days the king will arrive with ten legions, thirty thousand cavalry, a hundred thousand light-armed troops, three hundred elephants. Cease asking further questions and forming opinions for yourselves, and trust me who know; otherwise I shall put you on board a rotten ship, and send you forth at the mercy of the winds to some other country.' A few pages of selections from this biography ought to form part of the introduction to every edition of the *Bellum Gallicum*, so that those who read those campaigns at the beginning of their career in Latin may learn that there was a human side to the Cæsar whose exploits are narrated so impersonally in his own memoirs.

In the lives of Tiberius, Claudius, and Nero we can best observe Suetonius's interest in psychological development. Tacitus begins the *Annals* with the accession of Tiberius on the death of Augustus, and gives no satisfactory reasons to account for the sombre cruelty and suspicion which turned the latter part of his rule into a reign of terror. Tiberius's character remains an enigma in the *Annals*. The early pages of Suetonius's biography suggest that the explanation is to be found in the long years of his service under Augustus, when both the good and the bad elements in his character were thwarted or repressed in the interests of imperial ambition. Possessed of great qualities as a general and administrator, in the maturity of his powers he found himself nothing but a pawn in the hands of Augustus to establish the succession. Forced to divorce the wife he loved in order to marry the shameless Julia, then forced to retire to Rhodes and exposed to general contempt, cynically adopted and promoted by Augustus when all other hopes had failed, it is not surprising that on ascending the throne, at the age of fifty-five, his whole nature was warped and soured, and that he hated the society of Rome. The crop which Augustus sowed in craft Tiberius reaped in blood.

With Caligula or Caius, Claudius and Nero, we reach the culmination of the imperial madness. The influence of Christian tradition has secured for Nero the place of pre-eminence in that bad period, but his reign, though longer, was not more cruel or terrible than that of Caligula. The monstrous crimes actually committed during those reigns obscure all sense of distinction between fiction and truth, and no vice is too horrible, no excess too extravagant, to find a place in the imperial legend. Yet, though Suetonius accepts and repeats too lightly their long tale of horrors, though he too often mistakes the trivial or the vile for the interesting, he manages to preserve the element of reality in his presentation of them, and it is on this account that his biographies are a useful supplement to the ordinary histories of that period. His emperors possess character and life, in spite of his method, and bring an air of reality into the lifeless architecture of those archæological reconstructions with which guide-books and classical dictionaries clothe the Palatine Hill. He may be pedantic and monotonous in his collection and arrangement of facts, but in the actual writing he rises above these limitations, and the result is a curious and vivid work ; as vivid and as various as the gigantic remains which still encumber the Imperial Hill, vast arches and deep recesses, palace built beside palace, temple beside temple, refined Greek work lying among the coarse and ostentatious mouldings of Roman workmen. And even now the way up to the Palatine between soaring masses of brickwork has something gloomy and portentous about it, recalling the terrible figure of Caligula, who was murdered in one of those underground passages.

' He was tall,' Suetonius writes, ' and very pale, his body enormous, his neck and legs very thin, his eyes and temples hollow, his forehead broad and threatening, with but little hair upon his head and quite bald on the top, while everywhere else he was covered with hair . . . this horrible and savage appearance he used to render still more fearful by practising grimaces in front of a mirror.' And then he tells us how Caligula talked and quarrelled with Jupiter by night; how he built a bridge from the Palatine to the Capitol that he might enjoy more intimately the society of the god; how he was troubled with evil dreams, in the worst of which he seemed to be conversing with the sea (*pelagi quondam speciem conloquentem secum videre visus*); how he never slept more than three hours at night, and then used to wander up and down the long porticoes of the Palatine waiting for the dawn; how he used to show himself to the Romans, wearing a golden beard with the thunderbolt or trident or Mercury's wand in his hand, at other times in the dress and ornaments of the goddess Venus. Caligula is the only one of the emperors in whom Suetonius says there was a definite strain of madness of which the man himself was conscious. Judged in the light of ordinary standards, we should turn in disgust from him as a cruel madman, yet such was the terrible exaltation and power of an emperor that his wild claims and extravagant actions do not seem altogether inconsistent with his position or deprive him entirely of human interest and reality.

It was unfortunate that such an ancient family as the Julian should have been called on to supply the first emperors when, after so many centuries, the vitality of the stock was exhausted and the germs of decay firmly established in body and spirit. The evil first showed itself in Augustus's daughter Julia, and from her spread through the whole imperial household, infecting the Claudian family as well. The Emperor Claudius seems to have been marked from childhood with a perverse stupidity. We owe to Suetonius the preservation of a long extract from a letter of Augustus to his wife Livia, in which he says they ought to decide once and for all whether he is to be set aside as 'wanting in mind and body,' or advanced to the usual honours. In after years he complained of the severe treatment he received from his tutor, a barbarian groom. A sickly and backward boy, on growing to manhood he was continually set back at court, so that in Tiberius's reign he withdrew into private life, choosing for friends the most worthless men, and spending his time drinking and dicing. In the reign of Caius, his nephew, he returned to court, where, in spite of his middle age, he was exposed to mockery and horseplay at the imperial dinner parties. 'Whenever he fell asleep after dinner, as he often did, they used to throw olive and date-stones at him, and sometimes, to give amusement, the buffoons used to wake him up with a stick or a whip. And as he lay snoring, they used to put his slippers on his hands to watch him, when suddenly woken up, rub his face with them.' Yet the neglect with which he had been treated did not entirely spoil his character. His administration of the empire was not unsuccessful, but the extreme conscientiousness with which he attempted to discharge the emperor's duties was spoiled by the defects which he brought with him from his early life. Nervous and indecisive, learned and pedantic, slovenly and coarse in speech and dress, he was unable to maintain the imperial dignity whenever he had to say or do anything. 'In repose,' writes Suetonius, 'he was not without dignity of appearance; he was tall; his body well-proportioned, his neck strong; of handsome looks with white hair. But whenever he did anything seriously or in relaxation, many defects disfigured him; his laugh was ugly; if angry he foamed at the mouth; his nose ran; he stammered; and his head nodded ceaselessly.' Suetonius's account of Claudius is admirable. The introductory chapters contain all of the man's character that is necessary to understand his final development as emperor. We must not forget that Suetonius always imagines his readers to be in a position to read the standard histories of this period.

The closing years of Nero's reign are wanting in our text of Tacitus, and we cannot tell how closely Suetonius may have followed the great annalist. In other places where we can compare their accounts of the same incident, he does not appear to have copied Tacitus. Nor do we know if he has kept faithfully to any other historian, and in the present state of our knowledge we must accept his description of Nero's last days as a masterpiece of writing, whether it is viewed from the standpoint of psychology in the presentation of Nero's character or as an example of narrative.

> At Naples, on the anniversary of the day on which he had murdered his mother, Nero learned of the revolt in Gaul. He received the news with such calmness and indifference that he was suspected of being pleased at the chance of plundering those very rich provinces; he did not, however, defer a visit to the gymnasium, and watched with the keenest interest the practice of some athletes. Interrupted during dinner by more alarming dispatches, he became so angry that he threatened

vengeance upon the mutineers. During the next eight days he sent no reply to Rome, issued no commissions or commands, and passed over the matter in complete silence. At length the frequent and insulting edicts of Vindex forced him to urge the Senate to avenge himself and the state, while he excused his absence from Rome on the ground of a sore throat. What vexed him most of all was that Vindex derided him as a bad harp player. . . . But dispatch following dispatch, he returned in great anxiety to Rome ; on the journey he was cheered by a very trivial omen, a marble relief on a tomb showing a Roman Knight dragging by the hair a Gallic soldier ; he jumped to the ground in delight and did reverence to heaven. Arrived in Rome, he did not convene the Senate or the people, but summoned a few leading men to the palace, and after a hurried discussion spent the rest of the day examining new kinds of water organs, displaying each of them, discussing the construction and difficulties of each, and saying that he would exhibit them all in the theatre, if Vindex would kindly allow him.

And then in a succession of vivid scenes we can follow the stages of his swift passage from the fierce light of the throne into the darkness of a miserable death. He who a few days before had at his disposal all the men and resources of the empire suddenly found himself helpless and deserted in a silent palace. Disguised and accompanied by a eunuch and one or two freedmen, he left Rome by night, encompassed with the horror of impending death, perhaps a death of suffering, until in a wayside hovel, at the sound of pursuing horsemen, the necessary strength of will came to him to take his own life.

Some critics have asserted that Suetonius has no style. That is too harsh and sweeping a statement. The rhetorical periods of Cicero and Livy were no longer in fashion when Suetonius wrote. Nor has he the vigour and moral fervour kindled by indignation at the decay of Roman society which carries Tacitus so nobly through these evil years. The grand historical style would have been altogether unsuited to his matter. But he has developed a style for himself admirably adapted to this form of biography, in which he can narrate with the natural force of Latin in precise and flexible outline the events of each emperor's life, adding without rhetorical effort or undue emphasis outrageous gossip that has hardened into fact and facts so extravagant that they must assuredly be gossip. And on occasions Suetonius can rival the great historians in emotional brevity of form as well as in the deeper harmony and volume of utterance. What better instance could be found of stately and pathetic brevity of expression than in the words with which he describes the parting of Titus from his beloved Berenice? *Berenicen statim ab urbe dimisit, invitus invitam.* What hope is there of representing adequately and shortly in English those two last words of the Latin text? And in his characterisation of Nero there is this vast and sonorous sentence : *erat illi aeternitatis perpetuaeque famae cupido sed inconsulta.* 'He was possessed by an untimely longing for immortality and everlasting glory.' And how briefly and conclusively he suggests the tragic failure of Augustus's family life and his hope to found a dynasty : *aliquanto patientius mortem quam dedecora suorum tulit.* 'He found it more easy to endure death than disgrace in his family.' And in longer passages he can maintain a clear and vigorous narrative; the description of Vitellius's death is admirable and not at all inferior to that of Tacitus, and we have already mentioned the account of Nero's end as a masterpiece of writing, where he completely controls his material and achieves a harmonious form of real artistic power.

The age and vast extent of the Roman Empire was not a source of inspiration to Suetonius. He has no patriotic, no political feeling. He is at little pains to make us feel any indignation at the wickedness or folly of Caligula or Nero. Perhaps he felt that the bare record of their deeds was enough, but it is more likely that he had a leaning towards sensationalism, and he cannot altogether escape blame for dwelling too readily and at too great length upon the real or fictitious depravity

THE IMPERIAL LEGEND IN SUETONIUS

of Tiberius or Domitian. Had the other historians and writers of memoirs of that period survived, and particularly the sources which Suetonius used, we could dispense with him entirely. As matters are, he is a valuable and in certain points an indispensable supplement to Tacitus. We must be grateful to him for many things ; grateful for those unique descriptions of the personal appearance and way of life of the emperors ; grateful for the many *obiter dicta* which he has preserved, examples of the shrewd wit, the sound judgment, the grim and sometimes brutal humour so characteristic of the Romans, which never deserted even the feeblest or the maddest of the Twelve Cæsars ; grateful for all those vivid touches of personal detail, which break down the barriers of time and place and transport us into the presence of living men. How real does Augustus seem as we read Suetonius's account of the way he spent his days. We are indebted to him, too, for the preservation of passages from Augustus's letters, which afford us moments of direct vision, not only into the mind of the emperor, but into the life of the imperial household. He tells us of Julius Cæsar's banquets with Cleopatra, prolonged till dawn, while they sailed up the Nile through Egypt towards Aethiopia, until a mutiny of his troops forced him to turn back ; of Vespasian's last words, that an emperor ought to die standing up ; of Augustus's last words to his wife

Livia, bidding her 'remember their married life.' He records the Greek hexameter which Nero, so true to his rôle of artist, uttered before driving the knife into his throat ; the apt criticism of Caligula upon Seneca's prose style as being 'sand without lime,' and the sardonic humour of the same emperor in causing a new law to be posted up in such small letters that no one could read it ; the shrewd complaint of Claudius that he would be quite well off if only his freedmen would take him into partnership ; the caustic reply of Tiberius to the ambassadors from Troy, who were late in condoling with him on the death of his son Drusus, that 'he too offered them his condolences on the loss of their excellent citizen Hector.' He prepares us for the cruelty and madness of Domitian by telling us that 'at the beginning of his reign he spent several hours each day alone, doing nothing else but catching flies and transfixing them on a very sharp pen, so that a wit, on being asked if any one was with Cæsar, replied, 'No one, not even a fly.'

And just as nowadays the charm of flowers and trees and glimpses of the Sabine hills revive the visitor amid the sombre ruins and memories of imperial Rome, so there are touches of a gentler and finer humanity in the pages of Suetonius. He has troubled to record how year by year Nero's tomb was decked by unknown hands with spring and summer flowers ; he describes even more

THE IMPERIAL LEGEND IN SUETONIUS

effectively than Tacitus the calm ending of Otho's reckless life ; he tells us how the Emperor Vespasian loved to visit the humble villa where he had been born, allowing nothing to be changed there—*ne quid scilicet oculorum consuetudini deperiret* ; how he used his grandmother's simple silver mug on all days of solemn festival. He has rescued from oblivion the deep and long mourning of the Jews for Julius Cæsar, and the passionate love of Tiberius for his first wife, whom he was compelled by Augustus to divorce. His interest in the scandals and horrors and pitiful trivialities of the deified emperors has not blunted his feeling for the true values of mortality. *Sunt lacrimae rerum et mentem mortalia tangunt.*

This strange record of the sayings and actions of the Twelve Cæsars leaves an abiding impression of the crushing materialism and spiritual destitution of imperial Rome. Old temples were restored and new ones built, the ritual of worship was carried out in most rigorous form, but true Roman religious feeling was dead. The influence of the unseen was limited to superstition. The marble city into which Augustus boasted that he had transformed Rome was, in truth, only the mausoleum in which the Roman genius was laid to rest. The activity of endless spectacles and feasts, with its hopeless quest of material satisfaction, cannot be mistaken for the real process of life any more than the mechanical process of government continuing under good or bad emperors can be mistaken for healthy organic action. And Suetonius, though he writes in the assurance of a better age, from which the past century is receding like an evil dream, is still under the influence of the same superstitious materialism. He carefully recounts the dreams and omens and horoscopes which accompanied the birth, accession, and death of each emperor. These superstitious memories are very real to him and constitute all the divinity with which he can hedge his emperors. In the same vein he collects those utterances of theirs in which a prophetic spirit has been discerned, and then without any thought of inconsistency tells how these claimants to divine honours were terrified of thunderstorms and hid themselves in panelled rooms or under the bed. With the deification of the emperors the edifice of Roman materialism was complete, and nowhere can we feel the oppressive elaboration of its architecture better than in the pages of this baroque biographer.

CLASSICAL MYTHS IN THE NATIONAL GALLERY

→→←←

THE pictures in the National Gallery, whose subjects are taken from classical mythology, are among the most popular in the collection; some of that popularity is undoubtedly due to the relief given by such pictures from the continual repetition of religious themes in the Italian schools. In these 'profane' pictures the artist can be appreciated as artist or illustrator according to the inclination of the spectator without the intrusion of any religious or anti-religious sentiment. Some popularity is also aroused by recalling memories or providing illustrations in happier days of legends once familiar but unwelcome at school or college. To others the profound charm of those ancient legends, obscured in boyhood by the difficult triviality of Ovid's utterance, has been finally revealed by such a masterpiece as Titian's 'Bacchus and Ariadne.' Yet though these pictures may serve as illustrations, they are utterly free from the pedantic precision in archæological details which make illustrated editions of classical texts so futile and modern paintings of such subjects so sickly and valueless. If the spectator happens to be a classical scholar and has any feeling for art, he knows that archæological and artistic values must not be confused, and the general public, who are never quite sure if painting is anything more than the illustration of a subject, are of necessity quite indifferent to requirements of scholarship if only they can establish a general identity between title and treatment. And a similar indifference, springing, however, from a different cause, is characteristic of the Italian artists, even after editions of the classics and classical remains had become common in Italy. Antiquarianism was never allowed to cramp creative power, whereas in painters of inferior calibre it becomes the dominating influence in their work. Mantegna is the only great Italian artist to whom archæological truth was an obsession, and fortunately his genius was, in general, strong enough to mould his science into suitable artistic form.

Piero di Cosimo's 'Death of Procris'[1] is a good instance of the free handling by an artist of a familiar classical subject. Moore has turned the story into some pretty verses, and Ovid has told it at length in the *Art of Love* as well as in the *Metamorphoses*. Procris, jealous of her husband, follows him on a hunting expedition, betrays her presence by a movement in the thicket where she has concealed herself, and her husband, thinking the noise was caused by a wild beast, drew his bow at a venture and killed her. Piero

[1] N.G. 698.

IN THE NATIONAL GALLERY

was born about 1462, and the *editio princeps* of Ovid appeared in Rome in 1471, so that it is quite likely that he may have read the story for himself or heard an accurate version of it. And yet the picture is in no way a direct illustration of Ovid's verses, and those who do not know the classical story are not hindered in their enjoyment of the picture. It is antiquarian and illustrative in a peculiar manner. The dramatic moment of her death and discovery did not attract Piero. Procris is seen lying dead by the shore of an estuary in a wide, peaceful landscape where flowers and birds and dogs are shown with tender delicacy; the actual cause of her death is suggested or recalled to those who know by the presence in the foreground of the hunting dog and the satyr, a being in whom the life of the wilds is personified. The artist's emotions have been stirred not so much by the story as by the thought of the world in which the incident took place, by the freedom of that ancient life which he realises so convincingly in the landscape and in the figure of the satyr, while Procris remains a rather heavily conceived and executed form, just as clumsy as the nymphs in the same painter's picture of ' The Rape of Hylas.' [1] Piero had no power to present the beauty of the human form, but he conveys the tragic moment of death by the impressive form of the dog, gazing in

[1] Formerly in the collection of Mr. Robert Benson.

dumb sorrow at Procris, and by the exquisite delicacy of the half-human satyr laying his hands so gently, so humanly, upon the dead woman. The solemn stillness of the whole scene is only broken by a few birds quietly gliding down to the water in the background.

In his essay on Sandro Botticelli, Walter Pater has touched on that painter's peculiar treatment of the antique. 'You will find,' he says, referring to 'The Birth of Venus' in the Uffizi, 'that quaint design of Botticelli's a more direct inlet into the Greek temper than the works of the Greeks themselves of the finest period.' Botticelli, about whom Pater wrote so hesitatingly in 1870, almost apologising at the end of the essay for delaying so long upon a secondary painter, is now established as one of the greatest among Italian artists. Mr. Berenson calls him the 'greatest artist of lineal design that Europe has ever had,' at the same time drawing attention to Botticelli's general indifference to 'mere subject and representation': 'the secret is this, that in European painting there has never been an artist so indifferent to representation.' And it is consistent with this view of his genius that none of Botticelli's pictures are direct illustrations of a literary subject. The so-called 'Mars and Venus' in the National Gallery, 'The Birth of Venus' and 'The Spring' at Florence, are not based directly on any classical legends, but are

IN THE NATIONAL GALLERY

probably a free exercise upon some contemporary literary versification. In what way, then, is he so excellent ' an inlet into the Greek temper ' ? It is simply through his gift of design or orderly coherence. Design brings with it clearness of individual form, and subordination of the parts, not to a possible subject, but to the total effect. And that is the peculiar achievement of Greek art in the sixth and fifth centuries B.C. ; vases, reliefs on tombs, pediments of temples, all bear witness even in their ruin to a feeling for design, which must have been much more obvious in the undamaged brightness of marble and paint and metal. In the single statue it was on the effect of the whole that the artist concentrated, not on facial expression or graceful attitude ; in the pedimental groups he took the solid figure and repeated it to form an adequate design just as Botticelli throws together his figures in ' Spring ' or ' The Birth of Venus.' The Greek artist never allowed the power of the figures employed in the design to be diminished by charm of background or atmosphere, and they were always to be seen in the all-revealing light of Greece. The facial expression of Botticelli's figures is no more significant than the ' smile ' in early Greek sculpture ; his real interest is in the completed design, and in the service of that he has reduced the background of landscape to the most subordinate and conventional form, and placed his figures in a clear and austere light that has no enhancing or romantic effect on them. It is from these qualities that he is an 'inlet into the Greek temper.' There is in his work the same clearness and fragile delicacy of form that we can observe in the best Greek reliefs, for instance those on the famous Ludovisi throne in the National Museum at Rome, or dimmed by the copyist's hand but still triumphant in the 'Orpheus and Eurydice' at Naples, or that we can hear so often in the opening words of some chorus by Euripides :

σὺ μὲν, ὦ πατρὶς Ἰλιὰς,
τῶν ἀπορθήτων πόλις οὐκέτι λέξει.

Thou, O my country of Ilium,
Art no more counted a city unsacked. . . .

It is only by virtue of the descriptive title attached to it that Botticelli's 'Mars and Venus' in the National Gallery [1] can be counted 'classical' in content. A brief consideration of it is enough to convince one that it has very little directly illustrative matter in it. The artist may have received a suggestion from the beginning of Lucretius's poem, or, as some critics suggest, from a contemporary poet, Angelo Poliziano. The background of myrtle, the baby satyrs, themselves a variation by the painter on the virile classical type, are the only elements

[1] N.G. 915.

IN THE NATIONAL GALLERY

of the antique in the picture, though possibly the nude figure of the man is also due to its influence ; the armour, the costume of Venus are mediæval ; there is no great physical beauty in the figures such as we attribute to the gods and goddesses of Greece ; yet we feel the picture to be Greek in spirit because it is so clear and truthful in the realisation of every part, so free from all self-consciousness, so complete in its design, so dependent for its effect upon what is presented and nothing more.

Let us consider for a moment how far the pictures of Botticelli, which, though they are not illustrative of classical themes, at least contain a reference to that heroic world of legend, and the work of more directly illustrative painters, such as Piero di Cosimo and Titian, are an attempt to convey to the beholder something of the spirit which the artist, especially the Renaissance artist, felt about the dimly realised glory of ancient Greece and Rome. We must not forget that, by considering these pictures in such a manner, we are no longer viewing them as works of art in the strict sense of the term, impressing and delighting by form and colour, which alone are the decorative and essential moments of the art. We are taking them as illustrations which may charm us by the way in which they incorporate or suggest something of that beauty which the modern man, what-

CLASSICAL MYTHS

ever his education may have been, feels was the peculiar privilege of the creative imagination of the Greeks. The burden of translating the ancient texts may be still remembered, or may never have been experienced, yet all men, if they have any interest at all in the things of the spirit, regard the world of Homer and Pindar and the tragedians as a kind of fairyland in which men lived, gay or sad, as they have never again succeeded in living. For the mass of educated people, the classical world, curious and contradictory as it may seem, is really the romantic world, where the very clearness and reasonableness of form has become romantic to the blurred and indecisive vision of the modern mind. The present moment so often loses for us, as it did for the men of the Renaissance, all that sense of strangeness which is held to be an important element in romantic beauty. The society of the Renaissance turned from the awkward, sick, cramped forms of contemporary life to the vision of Greece conjured up by literature and the first archæological discoveries, as a life where beauty and freedom met together in perfect fusion. Vernon Lee probably gives a more truthful description of the society of the Middle Ages than Ruskin in his famous comparison between the burnished glory of Pisa and the noisome foulness of some Victorian Rochdale or Bradford.

IN THE NATIONAL GALLERY

> Large towns, in which thousands of human beings were crowded together in narrow, gloomy streets, with but a strip of blue visible between the projecting roofs. . . . Men and women pale and meagre for want of air, and light, and movement ; undeveloped, untrained bodies, warped by constant work at the loom or at the desk, at best with the lumpish freedom of the soldier and the vulgar nimbleness of the 'prentice . . . dressed in the dress of the Middle Ages, gorgeous perhaps in colour, but heavy, miserable, grotesque ; ladies in stiff and foldless brocade hoops and stomachers ; artizans in striped and close adhering hose and egg-shaped padded jerkin ; soldiers in lumbering armour-plates, ill-fitted over ill-fitting leather, a shapeless shell of iron . . . beside these there are lamentable sights, mediæval beyond words . . . dwarfs and cripples, maimed and diseased beggars . . . lepers and epileptics and infinite numbers of monks, brown, grey and black . . . emaciated with penance or bloated with gluttony.[1]

But the attraction of the antique world for artists was not only in its contrast with the sordid narrowness and deformity of contemporary life ; it was rather the complete freedom of movement which classical subjects gave them. Here was a material which they could mould and form according to their artistic desires, released from the limitations which the round of religious themes set upon them. Though great latitude was

[1] Vernon Lee, *Euphorion*, p. 190.

tolerated in religious painting, and public as well as artists were devoid of the self-conscious, archæological pedantry of the modern world, it was very rarely that an artist appeared whose artistic and religious vision coincided. In the case of Botticelli, whose interest in the subject was trifling, the freedom made possible by combining forms from the antique world must have been most welcome. None of his religious pictures are artistically so satisfying as those masterpieces 'Pallas taming the Centaur' and 'The Birth of Venus.'

Yet, while the classical world and all that recalled it was essentially romantic to the mind of that age, Botticelli stands almost alone by not being romantic in his mode of treatment. Tintoretto is the only other artist of the Renaissance who agrees with him in this respect. The rest invest their presentations of the antique world with an atmosphere charged with marvels, possessing something dæmonic, which we no longer find in the light of common day. Think, for instance, of Titian's 'Bacchus and Ariadne,'[1] one of the most splendid and famous pictures in the National Gallery. There is nothing here of the clear form and austere light of Botticelli. The landscape and figures have nothing of the essential Greek spirit about them. The picture impresses us as a whole by the intensity of its colour and action, an event in a world where

[1] N.G. 35.

everything has the vitality of heroic life. And
the influence of a wider knowledge of the Latin
poets makes itself felt in the wealth and accuracy
of detail ; the rich pageant of mythology as we
know it in Ovid's *Metamorphoses* and *Fasti*, but
without the polished incredulity and rhetoric of
the Latin writer, has been absorbed into Titian's
work. Imagination can only speak to imagination, and the meeting of Bacchus and Ariadne
may have risen before Catullus's mind's eye in
the form which Titian has given to it.

The ' Venus and Adonis,' which has been
cleaned recently with such success and vindi-
cated as worthy of Titian, belongs to a much
later period in the artist's life, and may have
been painted when he was over seventy. The
contrast between his mode of expression in this
picture and in ' Bacchus and Ariadne,' painted
thirty years before, is great. The intense imaginative colouring of the younger Titian has disappeared. The mythological element is very
slight and unobtrusive : Venus drives her chariot
through the sky and Cupid lies asleep beneath
the trees in the background. The freedom, the
directness, and the simplicity of this representation bring it much closer to the Greek spirit,
entirely satisfied with the beauty of the male and
female form as the material for a noble design.
The muscular figure of Adonis recalls the Greek
god of war rather than the ' tender boy ' of

Shakespeare's poem. One cannot help feeling that the Titian of this period was the greater artist.

Tintoretto is another great Venetian painter who has left us several pictures of classical subjects. The two famous pictures—the 'Bacchus and Ariadne' and the 'Hermes and the Three Graces'—in the Ducal Palace are well known to every visitor to Venice. These works show that Tintoretto, though in very different fashion, was no less a perfect interpreter of the antique world than Botticelli. Tintoretto dwells upon the beauty of physical form and superhuman vitality ; he does not use the colour of Titian ; there is very little direct classical allusion ; the vine and the stars in the 'Bacchus and Ariadne' are reduced to purely decorative values. Yet if one wished to find in painting the equivalent of the grand female figures on the pediments of the Parthenon, it is to these works that one should turn. Their forms are more than human, and the life that pulsates so intensely in them, sometimes in repose as in 'The Ariadne,' or rousing itself as in 'The Three Graces,' belongs to a form of the world that has for ever passed away. These pictures are tremendous as works of art without any reference to their subject ; as illustrations they conjure up for us that heroic life which the historical Greeks imagined to be spread about the infancy of their race.

IN THE NATIONAL GALLERY

The National Gallery has the good fortune to possess one such picture by Tintoretto ;[1] it is 'The Origin of the Milky Way,' a splendid example of the master's power in design and colour, so magnificent indeed that here, for once, is a picture more often admired for its artistic qualities than for its illustrative value. Comparisons in the arts are hateful as death to many people, but it is the spirit in which he conceives his design that makes one think of Pindar in looking at this masterpiece. There is the same magnificent richness and impetuosity of imagination in both artists. Those who have read Pindar, and every now and then through the difficulties of vocabulary and transitions of thought have suddenly seen the wonder of his poetry in some passionate outburst of language, will recognise in Tintoretto a kindred genius of the lyrical type. The splendour of life is as evident in the design of Tintoretto as in the Epinikian odes, where colour and speed and fineness of imagery in thought and word are blended into an astonishing arabesque. An echo of the original magnificence remains even in translation.

> For he—the babe Iamus—was hidden among rushes and in an impenetrable brake, his tender body all suffused with golden and deep purple

---

[1] N.G. 1313.

CLASSICAL MYTHS

> gleams of iris flowers . . . but when he had come to the ripeness of golden-crowned, sweet youth he went down into the middle of the river Alpheos and called on wide-ruling Poseidon . . . and he stood beneath the heavens and it was night.[1]

and of the start of the Argonauts :

> Then their chief, taking in his hands a golden goblet, stood up upon the stern and called on Zeus whose spear is the lightning and on the rush of waves and winds and the nights and paths of the deep. . . . And from the clouds a favourable voice of thunder pealed in answer ; and there came bright lightning flashes bursting through.[2]

Tintoretto, as well as Botticelli, is an 'inlet,' though by a very different method, 'into the Greek temper.' Botticelli interprets the early and unspoiled artistic genius of Greece ; Tintoretto reveals to us their ideals of physical beauty and life. He transmits to us through his figures their passionate zest for life and beauty realised in vitality of form rather than in any peculiarity of expression. His type of women is regal but impersonal ; their looks are grave and regular ; such women could only be the mothers of demigods and heroes. Tintoretto possesses the gift of direct imaginative insight on a grand scale and the power to create form, and by these gifts, without any archæological knowledge of the

[1] Myers.   [2] *Ibid.*

antique world, can naturally reveal to us the spirit of a people whose vision of the world was absolutely direct, undimmed by any tradition or bias inherited from elsewhere. These two artists, by their independence of thought, stand outside the influence of Roman civilisation which the heavier and more sensuous nature of Titian, and still more of Correggio,[1] could not altogether escape. They feel the necessity of creating a special atmosphere of romance or charm for the presentation of the antique ; there is no trace of such ' staging ' in the work of Botticelli and Tintoretto. The lesser artists, such as Pintoricchio[2] or Benozzo Gozzoli,[3] have not even that power of romantic atmosphere, and depict ' The Rape of Helen ' or the ' Return of Odysseus ' in Ovidian fashion ; the figures are pretty or quaint or debonair, conceived without the least emotion, animated by nothing more substantial than trivial rhetoric. Among these lesser artists Boltraffio is a remarkable exception. The peculiarity of his genius seems for once to be exactly suited by such a theme as ' Narcissus,'[4] in which he has expressed in highly individual fashion the dreamlike charm of the beautiful legend.

If the Dutch and Flemish masters felt the attraction of the antique world, they suggest

[1] N.G. 90, ' The Education of Cupid.'   [2] N.G. 911.
[3] N.G. 591.   [4] N.G. 2673.

CLASSICAL MYTHS

little of it in those pictures which have classical titles. Rembrandt is romantic in the modern sense of the term, and the ' Diana Bathing '[1] in the National Gallery is only a study of light and shade effects on a nude in water. Rubens either exaggerates the antique element beyond all recognition as in his Satyrs[2] or places uncomfortable nudes in an elaborate landscape and calls it ' The Judgment of Paris.'[3] There is no sympathetic relation between the conception and form of such works and the reference given by the title ; they have no illustrative element in them, and it is precisely the lack of those essential Greek qualities, clearness of design and restraint, which so often prevents Rubens's work from being great art.

' Classical myths ' reappear largely in the works of two great French artists of the seventeenth century, Poussin and Claude Gellée. Their lives were mostly spent in Italy, and in an age of classical pedantry they were saved by the strength of their genius from being academically antiquarian. The artists of the Renaissance had been inspired by the freedom and beauty of the ancient life ; Poussin and Claude were inspired by the ruins of the past, and that past belonged to Rome rather than to Greece ; they viewed the past through the Renaissance with its high hopes and ruined remains dug from the earth,

[1] N.G. 2538.   [2] N.G. 853.   [3] N.G. 194.

IN THE NATIONAL GALLERY

and its failure. The pictures of Claude,[1] in which a group of figures is placed in a landscape with classical buildings or ruins, possess the meditative calm and pathos of Virgil ; in that serene and spacious atmosphere the life of the world is suspended, and we feel only the significance of the past in which this particular spot may have been the scene of some great issue. His famous ' Enchanted Castle ' is symbolic of all his pictures ; the figures in them are powerless to make them anything but landscapes, impressive and artistic by their feeling for space beneath an infinite sky, yet sometimes cloying from an excess of classical sentiment in the buildings, or idyllic calm in the evening light.

The genius of Poussin is much more profound and vigorous than that of Claude. Claude was unable to paint the human figure ; Poussin is completely master over it, and had great power of design as well. His landscape is intense and primeval ; his colour is often harsh and strange, striking a constant note of dissonance in his work ; his figures have the regular beauty of Greek sculpture. He always remains curiously aloof from his subject, as though he were quite indifferent to or uninspired by it, and accepted classical or biblical themes from the necessity of tradition rather than of free choice. He is a

[1] N.G. 2, 19.

pure artist, free from illustrative or romantic desires, sadly hampered by the conventions of the past, Cupids, Hermes, and empty gestures, and the academic demands of the present. It is curious to find Hazlitt, in his essay on ' A Landscape of Nicolas Poussin,' saying that ' no one ever told a story half so well.' Hazlitt spoke for the cultured class of his age, who were saturated in the Latin poets at school, and he probably contributed from his own memory five-sixths of the story which he thought Poussin was telling so well. Poussin is dramatic and tragic, but he is no illustrator in the ordinary sense; he realises a significant moment by the dignity of his form and design; he often makes it poignant by the peculiarity of his colour; ' the learned indifference of his colour,' Hazlitt calls it. These qualities can be enjoyed by the ordinary spectator, who would be sadly troubled to fill out the story of such masterpieces as ' Cephalus and Aurora '[1] in the National Gallery or ' Armida and Rinaldo ' at Dulwich. Poussin is incredulous about the joy and freedom and reality of the antique. His Satyrs and Nymphs ' have more of the intellectual part of the character and seem vicious on reflection and of set purpose . . . with bodies less pampered than Rubens's, but with minds more secretly depraved'; their dances are joyless in spite of the

[1] N.G. 65.

IN THE NATIONAL GALLERY

vitality of their forms, and the descriptive title —'Happiness subject to Death'—which Bellori gave to the picture of 'Shepherds in Arcadia' is profoundly true of all his work except the landscapes. His genius is most harmonious in landscape,[1] solemn and tragic like the country of the great Roman poets Lucretius and Virgil, pregnant with the mysterious presence of Pan and the spirits of lonely woodlands.

Most visitors to the National Gallery know Turner's 'Ulysses deriding Polyphemus';[2] it is the apotheosis of the romantic vision of the ancient world in which, contrary to all their conceptions of art and life, man has dwindled away to almost nothing in the scene and the elements of nature are supreme. Amid the gorgeous hues and clouds of early morning is the ship of Ulysses, a marvellous galley, with the hero himself, a very small figure, upon it, while amid the mist upon a mighty mountain's side the dim form of the giant can be discerned. All that colour can do to make a given moment infinitely suggestive has been done, and the picture really gives the glamour of the sea, the romance of adventure in a wonderful world:

> There's a schooner in the offing,
>   With her topsails shot with fire,
> And my heart has gone aboard her
>   For the Islands of Desire.

---

[1] N.G. 40.   [2] N.G. 508.

CLASSICAL MYTHS

Those who approach Greek art or literature in their earlier manifestations, with conceptions formed or suggested by the countless painters who have taken their subject-matter from Greek legend, find themselves often 'moving about in worlds not realised.' For Turner, as for Titian, the simple form or event by itself is not enough; they are romantic in temperament. The Greeks, until their nerve began to fail after the Peloponnesian war, cared only for clear and carefully realised form; they had an uncompromising preference for what was natural and real, and for the beauty of the human body; they were nervous and suspicious of nature; they were indifferent to 'sunset effects'; they preferred the steady sunlight of full morning or afternoon, the dispeller of illusions, typified by Plato as the fountain of truth and knowledge on earth; and in the same clear light they saw the forms and actions of their own legendary past.

WINCKELMANN IN ROME

NOT far from one of the busiest streets in the new quarter of Rome beyond the Pincian Hill, where speculators in the tourist traffic have built imposing hotels for the elaborate entertainment of the modern visitor, a glimpse can be caught through iron gates of the gardens of the Villa Albani. Erected in the middle of the eighteenth century for Cardinal Alessandro Albani, the nephew of Pope Clement XI., it long combined the attraction of being close to the city with the charm of a country residence, with elaborate gardens and a wonderful view across the Campagna to the Sabine hills, until the expansion of Rome enclosed it with buildings on all sides. Probably few of the visitors who frequent the hotels in its neighbourhood are even aware of the existence of the Villa Albani. Lovers of the old masters know that the villa contains a beautiful triptych by Perugino, and students of ancient sculpture hold it sacred to the memory of Johann Joachim Winckelmann.

The name of Winckelmann and something of his life are known to many from the essay in Walter Pater's *Renaissance* ; and some, perhaps, may have recalled those admirable pages, during their travels, on chancing to notice in the Gallery of Ancient Sculpture at Munich an attractive faun's head in marble, which is still called Winckelmann's Faun, because it was once his cherished possession in Rome ; or else, detained in Trieste, as he was long ago, may have been reminded of his history by seeing the monument set up to honour his memory in that city. There can, indeed, hardly be a better testimony to the artistic power of Pater's writing than the fact that the few pages devoted to Winckelmann in that essay do not easily pass away from the memory, and leave with many an abiding impression of having been in communion with a real personality, able to arouse and purify intellectual effort and to enforce by its example the supreme value of singleness of purpose in things of the spirit.

The best record of Winckelmann's life and personality is contained in his letters, where he reveals directly not only his artistic and intellectual enthusiasms but also the charm of his humanity in the incidents and emotions of daily life. The volume of selections [1] from them, edited by Uhde-Bernays as a companion volume to a reprint of Winckelmann's *Essays*, is an excellent substitute for the complete edition, which has been long out of print, and spares the reader the necessity of toiling through much technical

[1] *Kleine Schriften und Briefe*. Insel Verlag, Leipzig, 1925.

matter connected with printing and plates. A few more letters from the later Roman period would have been acceptable, but, in general, the selection is admirable, and Goethe's appreciation of Winckelmann forms an excellent introduction to the first volume.

Writing from Rome to his friend Marpurg in 1762, Winckelmann says :

> I can briefly summarise my early life. I was co-rector of the school at Seehausen for seven and a half years ; librarian to Count Bünau at Dresden for a similar period, and lived for one year by myself at Dresden before my journey to Rome. . . . There you have the life of Johann Winckelmann, born at Stendal in the Altmark at the beginning of the year 1718 [the actual date was December 9, 1717].

His real life he counted as only beginning with his arrival in Rome, and he goes on :

> I am now in the eighth year of my life, for so long have I resided in Rome and other towns of Italy. Here I have tried to recall my youth which I lost partly in unruliness, partly in hard work and misery, and I shall die at least more contented, for I have gained all my wishes, yes, more than I could have thought, hoped for, or deserved.

On November 18, 1755, after a journey from Dresden lasting eight weeks, Winckelmann arrived in Rome. He took lodgings in a house much frequented by students of painting, ' Alla

Trinità dei Monti,' above the Piazza di Spagna —already a favourite quarter for foreigners—' in the healthiest part of Rome near the Villa Medici, and from my window I have a view over the whole of Rome right away to the sea.' He brought with him a letter of introduction to Anton Raphael Mengs, the well-known painter, who had been living in Rome for the past ten years, since his appointment as Court painter to the King of Poland. During the first year of his residence in Rome, Winckelmann saw much of Mengs, who lived close beside him; he dined with him frequently, and spent the evenings in discussions about the mysteries of art.

The allowance which Winckelmann was receiving from the King of Poland was enough to provide him with the necessaries of life, and he proudly refused to thrust himself upon the attention or to ask favours of Cardinal Archinto, who, as Nuncio at Dresden, had received Winckelmann into the Roman Church. In 1755 Archinto was very powerful in Rome as Secretary of State to Benedict XIV., and there was a possibility that he might himself become Pope before long. In order to have access to a good library, Winckelmann procured an introduction to Cardinal Passionei, who had also been active on his behalf at the time of his conversion; and he now found in Passionei his first influential friend in Rome. After the stiff pedantry of German officials and courtiers, Winckelmann was delighted to experience the easy courtesy of Roman manners, where personal merit and learning secured the respect and friendship of men of high birth and position.

In January 1756, through the influence of Bianconi, Court physician at Dresden, Winckelmann was received in audience by the Pope. This honour improved his position in Rome, for society did not know how influential his connections and support might be. His growing intimacy and public appearances with Cardinal Passionei at length aroused Archinto from his indifference, and in 1757 he offered Winckelmann rooms in the Cancelleria. After some delay, to show his independence, he accepted the Cardinal's offer, and voluntarily began to set in order the library without making any stipulation about salary. Quietly and steadily he won the consideration and friendship of the learned and artistic circle of Roman society, and within two years of his arrival he felt his position assured and could write to a friend, Genzmar, as follows :

> Although I have refused employment with Cardinal Passionei, he has become my greatest friend. . . . I have free access to his library and can get any books I want from it. I dine with him when I like and go with him to his charming country house, where I have just enjoyed for six weeks the delights of autumn in the society of

Cardinals and learned men. The liberty which the Cardinal allows is so great that one can appear at meals in dressing-gown and bonnet. . . . As the Cardinal is seventy-seven years old and I must have a patron whose prospect of life is longer, I took up my residence over a year ago with Cardinal Archinto, Secretary of State, in the Palace of the Cancelleria, but nothing more than that. Of my own accord I have set in order his large library and enjoy the use of it. Whenever I like I go and dine with the Cardinal, yet only with the purpose of pleasing him, without any prejudice to my freedom, which I intend to maintain jealously, seeing I am just on forty.

Winckelmann spent the second half of 1758 in Florence, engaged on a catalogue of the gems in the late Baron von Stosch's collection, whose heir, Philip Muzel-Stosch, became from this time Winckelmann's chief correspondent and friend. The Baron had recognised Winckelmann's knowledge and artistic insight from his first publication at Dresden, and there had been an interchange of letters, culminating in his choice of Winckelmann as artistic executor in the matter of his gems; and he also conferred another benefit of far-reaching material value for Winckelmann by giving him an introduction to Cardinal Albani, which bore fruit while he was actually engaged on the catalogue. During that autumn Archinto had a stroke and died almost immediately, and Winckelmann found

WINCKELMANN IN ROME

himself without a home or patron in Rome. His anxiety about the future did not last long. The news of Archinto's death was quickly followed by a letter from Giacomelli, the most learned prelate in Rome, with whom Winckelmann had read Dante, in which he conveyed an offer from Albani of rooms in his palace and a yearly allowance. Winckelmann accepted the offer without hesitation and, secure against material worries, could proceed to execute what he had long felt to be his life's task, the History of Ancient Art.

The duties and new way of life which this change brought with it are described by Winckelmann in a letter to Berendi :

> I am librarian to Cardinal Alessandro Albani, with a salary of five zecchins a month, without having to do a stroke of work either for him or in the library. I only have to drive out with him at his side. Our intimacy is so great that I sit on his bed and chatter to him there. He would gladly have me with him at meals, but that is hardly possible, for he dines with Prince Albani and the two Princesses. But when we are in his villas, that difficulty is removed. . . . In the evening I accompany the Cardinal into the society of a lady who has been a beauty. He remains there till midnight, and I go home about one o'clock or take supper in some friend's house. I get up at four in the morning, sleep soundly like a child, without waking up or sweating, as I used to do. I

> have an apartment of four rooms in the Cardinal's palace, quiet and charming, in the finest position in Rome. I work like a hero.

The methodical habits which he formed during his early years in Germany remained all his life, and the distractions of Roman society could not divert him from his settled purpose of hard work. For the greater part of the year he lived in the Albani Palace in Rome ; during the summer months he moved with the Cardinal to his villa. ' Every morning before sunrise I am on the flat roof of the palace to watch the day break in the East.' The villa became for the time the Court of Rome, and the Pope was a regular visitor every year. We hear several times of the gay and distinguished society gathered together there, of dinner parties of thirty and forty guests, followed by dancing till daylight ; and in 1764 the gaiety became so wild that the Pope expressed his displeasure, and ' the mad villegiatura ' came to a sudden end.

In April 1763 Winckelmann was appointed Antiquary to the Apostolic Chamber, or Inspector in Chief of the antiquities of Rome and the neighbourhood. Shortly afterwards he received a position as ' writer ' in the Vatican, which he resigned in 1767, as it took up too much of the valuable morning hours. At last he found his merits recognised and his fame established. Rome had become his fatherland—' the land of humanity,' he called it—and he expected to end his life there. The years passed by full of work. His official duties were not exacting. The Stosch catalogue, written in French, had been published in 1760; and thereafter his letters show him ceaselessly occupied, first with the History of Ancient Art, which, after many vexations and much rewriting, appeared at the end of 1763; then with collecting material and plates for the two volumes of *Monumenti Inediti*, published in April 1767. In addition to this private work, it fell to his lot, as head of the department of antiquities and the possessor of an international reputation, to show to distinguished visitors or travellers, who came with letters of introduction to him, the sights and art treasures of Rome. He often complains of the waste of time which this involved, and mentions with supreme indignation a young Englishman who regarded all the most beautiful works of art that were shown to him with an impassive and expressionless stare. But where he found interested and intelligent listeners, such as the young German princes of Anhalt-Dessau, Brunswick, and Mecklenburg, who were in Rome during 1765-66, Winckelmann, the divinely gifted teacher and passionate disciple of Plato, delighted to awaken the love of the beautiful that was slumbering in their souls.

It is one of the peculiar attractions of archæology that it draws its students into the open air and the society of other men, and forces them to move from place to place. All his life Winckelmann had a passion for planning voyages ; and the year before his death he was full of thoughts about an archæological expedition to Elis. He visited Naples four times ; he tells us also in his letters of visits to Cardinal Spinelli in his villa at Ostia, where he discovered a large bas-relief ; to Cardinal Stoppani at Palestrina, who knew Horace by heart, and was ready to make Winckelmann a yearly allowance from his own purse to prevent him from accepting a position in Berlin. On December 10, 1766, he writes to Count von Schlabrendorf that he is going to stay at Nettuno with Cardinal Corsini : 'Does not your mouth water, dear friend, when I talk to you about a visit to the sea-coast, especially when it is the coast of the Mediterranean, where even in winter there is an eternal spring?' With zest, yet without any grossness, he records his delight in drinking freely of the Roman wines, in eating the Roman broccoli or the Neapolitan cauliflowers ; in 1764, at Naples, he laments that he can no longer drink the Lagrima in the same measure as on earlier visits. The memory of the hardship and dreariness of his early years made him doubly sensitive to the rich privileges of his Roman sojourn. 'Each morning I spend half an hour thinking over my good fortune. I sing hymns from my Lutheran

WINCKELMANN IN ROME

hymn-book, and am happier than the Great Mogul.'

He tasted to the full the consciousness of good health, of sound sleep, of being able to see and to work wherever he was. In April 1767 he writes from Porto d'Anzio :

> I get up before daybreak, light a fire of myrtle wood, which is very plentiful here, and make my cup of chocolate. I read for three hours, then go for a walk along the shore or past the pleasant villas on the cliffs. At midday I enjoy an excellent dinner in the company of an elderly lady who is ready for any kind of society. Then, if I feel inclined to sleep, I can take a siesta.

The appreciation of nature is one of the traits in Winckelmann's character which differentiates him sharply from the mass of his educated contemporaries. As in art he turned from the over-elaborate artificiality of the day to the noble simplicity of Greek beauty, which he divined rather than saw in the remnants of sculpture in Rome, and as his daily and yearly life was lived in the same simple and noble manner, so he found in the landscape at Frascati or Castel Gandolfo, in ' the birth of some chance morning or evening among the Sabine hills,' or on the coast of Latium, the same noble and satisfying simplicity. He saw in the lines of the Roman landscape that spirit of delicate beauty which he felt in the best art of antiquity or in good Greek printing, where 'the grace of the letters depends on an almost imperceptible rise and fall, swelling and diminution in their formation. This slight variation is not perceptible to every one, and is the distinction of the master in every form of art.' It is not surprising, then, to learn that he, who was so sensitive to delicacy of line, should prefer the Roman and Florentine landscape to the Neapolitan. 'As soon as you have passed out of the lonely and desolate district round Rome you are in the most glorious country in the world. The natural beauty is indescribable.'

The Italian sunlight, the atmosphere of spring days, delighted him no less than the landscape. He equates his physical with his spiritual experiences. 'Your letters,' he writes to Usteri, 'are like days in spring, the longer they are the more delightful and beautiful they are.'

From Castel Gandolfo he writes:

> I am enjoying this heavenly spot, which surpasses everything in the world.... I am staying for a few weeks at one of the beautiful villas of my patron in a district which Omnipotence and the source of the knowledge of the highest beauty could not have made more beautiful.... I am alone in the country which you saw so hurriedly. I enjoy a life seasoned with intellectual pleasures and shall remain here till September.

In February 1768—the last year of his life—

he writes from Porto d'Anzio to Franke, at Dresden:

> This is the place of my happiness and I wish I could see you here, my friend, and could walk with you in free and leisurely fashion along the peaceful shore, or, when it is windy and rough, watch calmly the sea from an arch of the ancient temple of Fortune or from the balcony of my room. . . . Mind and heart are both strengthened by the enjoyment of the beauty of nature and art, which surpasses the brilliance of courts and their noisy riot.

And then, as he himself says, like ' a walker with light step and cheerful spirit,' he passes from out of the clearness and serenity of the Italian landscape into the threatening gorges of Tirol and the mists of the North, to see once more his friends in Germany before finally settling down in Rome. He did not realise how soon ' the continual cheerfulness which the Roman climate bestows ' would fail him beneath a different sky. The prospect of seeing friends at the end of his journey made him underestimate the physical strain of so much travelling at his age amid people from whose language and manners he had become estranged, through countries unrelieved by the brightness and beauty of the South, and without the prospect of artistic discoveries to stimulate him. The sheltered life which he had led in Rome for the last twelve years had unfitted him for continual movement, for the worries and physical discomforts of miserable inns and rough roads, for the melancholy arrivals in strange places at nightfall with the same prospect in view for the following day. His nerve gave way under the strain, and at Vienna he decided to hurry back to Italy.

> This journey [he writes on the 14th of May 1768, in his last letter to Muzel-Stosch] has brought with it deep depression instead of cheerfulness; and as I cannot make it in the necessary comfort nor do so in the future, it has lost all pleasure for me and I see no other way to recover my spirit than by returning to Rome. From Augsburg onwards I have tried in every possible way to force myself to be cheerful; but my heart refuses and my dislike of all this travelling is invincible. The delight of resting in your house, my friend, would be very short, and on my return journey I should have to stop in countless towns and just so often have to begin life over and over again. Be patient, my friend. Now that my intense longing has turned to bitterness, I am convinced that I can hope for no real pleasure outside Rome, if it has to be bought with such countless discomforts. . . . My friend, I should like to write much more, but I am not as I should wish to be. I want to start in a few days with the stagecoach for Trieste and from there reach Ancona by sea.

WINCKELMANN IN ROME

On June 8 he was murdered in his room at an inn in Trieste by a common thief.

Pater justifies the inclusion of an essay on Winckelmann in a volume of studies on the Renaissance on the ground that he really belongs in spirit to an earlier age. By his enthusiasm for the things of the intellect and the imagination for their own sake, by his Hellenism, his lifelong struggle to attain to the Greek spirit, he is in sympathy with the humanists of an earlier century. He is the last fruit of the Renaissance and explains in a striking way its motives and tendencies. It can be reasonably urged in opposition that all scholars in whom the passion for truth and freedom in knowledge burns brightly are in sympathy with the humanists of the Renaissance, but that the possession of that spirit is not enough in itself to bring the possessor within the limits of that earlier century. Is it not permissible to regard him as a rebel against the conventional attitude of pedantry into which the intellectual enthusiasm of the Renaissance had become frozen, and against the frigid artificiality and exaggeration of the first half of the eighteenth century? The force that carried Winckelmann through that hard period of probation in Germany was his passionate desire for personal and intellectual freedom, realised for him in the beauty of simple and sincere forms of life or art, such as friendship and

Greek sculpture. The life and art of Greece as he saw it, first of all through literature, and then through the better Roman copies of Greek statues, possessed a natural truth and simplicity, a reality of feeling, which were altogether wanting in the fashions of European life and art of his period. Even the placid insipidity and the unrelieved plainness of feebler Roman work, monotonously executed for villas and gardens, may have possessed an emancipating value for an eye that revolted from the emotionalised drapery and exaggerated attitudes of the school of Bernini.

But if he was in one sense a rebel and a heretic in refusing to bow down before the artistic idols of his day, he was also an initiator and a teacher working by specific precept and fullness of knowledge in his own day and by the example of devotion to his ideal on subsequent generations. Hegel has said of him that he opened a new sense for the appreciation of the antique ; rather he swept away the obstructions which had obscured that sense and enabled men to use it freely. From him, too, flows the spirit of modern archæology, that harmonious union of knowledge and observation, of scientific method and passionate feeling, which has been the mark of all great and successful workers in that field. The appearance of his History of Ancient Art marks the

WINCKELMANN IN ROME

beginning of a new period. Writing to Gessner, he says :

> It is indeed time, after nearly three hundred years, that some one should attempt a systematic history of ancient art, not with the purpose of improving our art, which is possible only for very few of those who practise it, but to learn to observe and admire the art of the ancients. Vague expressions are of no use here ; teaching must be precise and based on definite laws.

These last words show plainly enough that his enjoyment of art was no vague and undifferentiated admiration of what was ' classical.' His initiation is the severe one of methodic training and scholarly purification ; and that is his great legacy to students of ancient art. Goethe's remark about Winckelmann, that ' one learns nothing from him but one becomes something,' expresses in epigrammatic manner his function as an initiator. His history of art, his shorter writings and letters, are still read and valued, not for any practical results, but because a living spirit moves in them. The reader will not learn from them the adroit handling of facts, or fresh points of view or interpretation. He will be exposed to a transforming force ; he will experience something more rare and precious than the example of massive erudition or luminous exposition. He will have been brought close to the fire of a master spirit who, within his own limits, strove for fullness of knowledge without narrowing the range or blunting the fine edge of his æsthetic perceptions, whose life by the final harmony of its inner and outer form approximates to a work of art and exercises the stirring and compelling power of such things. It is upon this aspect of Winckelmann's significance that Herder dwells in the earliest appreciation of him that we possess.

In his introduction to the letters, Uhde-Bernays joins Winckelmann with Hölderlin and Marées, a poet and a painter, to form a trinity of great German Hellenes. The juxtaposition is apt and interesting. Hölderlin and Marées are creative artists. Winckelmann is primarily an interpreter of art ; but there are many passages in his writings where his feelings kindle and burn brightly at the inspiration of ancient art, and he too becomes an artist and achieves power of form. In virtue of this gift he is more than the forerunner of all modern Hellenes : he is the inspired prophet of Greek art. His actual work was that of a pioneer, fundamental and, to later generations, elementary, yet none the less precious. He cleared the ground and marked it out for others. Hölderlin and Marées may be greater artists, but they are lesser men than Winckelmann.

The richness and broadness of Winckelmann's humanity is most clearly seen in his practice of friendship. 'Friendship without love,' he writes, 'is mere acquaintance.' All his life he craved for true friendship, as he writes to von Berg, by 'an incomprehensible attraction, which is not solely due to beauty of form and feature, but to the working of that harmony which passes understanding and is attuned to the eternal unity of all things.' The perfect freedom and equality of such friendship, with its mysterious power of self-sacrifice, he felt to be divine, to be but another form of the beautiful. 'To realise to oneself such a friend as you are is to raise oneself to the verge of the divine—a piece of good fortune which is not granted to the great ones of the world.' He even felt that the perfect contentment of such a friendship might draw man away from God. In a curious passage in a letter to Franke, regretting the coldness of their intercourse at Nöthenitz, he says :

> In that I recognise the counterweight belonging to all human things. Ability has its portion of indifference, and those who are naturally inclined for friendship, and might find in it the highest human happiness, such as it is, are yet prevented by fancies of their own creation from finding in it that perfect contentment which must be sought in God alone.

The unifying power in his life was his desire of the beautiful, in which his religious as well as his æsthetic needs were satisfied. His passion to enjoy the beautiful and to communicate it to others spread from his central enthusiasm for Greek art over the rest of his life, urging him constantly to develop his relationships towards the external world of men and of nature into definite perceptions of beauty. The regulative principle of his outer as of his inner life was his love of freedom. But that love was preserved from caprice or extravagance by his innate feeling for form—that is, limit and law. 'The law shall make you free'; and Winckelmann's ardent quest of freedom is based on, and justified by, his self-imposed obedience to the law of beauty. This union of freedom and law is the secret of his tonic influence on all who follow with care the stages of his life. 'The noble freedom which I have laboriously hunted down' was no liberty to lead the careless existence of artistic enjoyment; it was freedom to develop the power which he was conscious he possessed, and to help others to experience in art and nature and friendship the divine as well as the beautiful. Quite soon after his arrival in Rome he wrote: 'I believe I have come here to help a little in opening the eyes of those who will visit Rome in days to come.' And in truth he is much more than an inspiring guide to the 'calm and noble beauty' of Greek sculpture; he typifies the spirit in which Rome should be approached, an eagerness to enter into and appreciate all the manifold forms of its beauty, tempered by a sense of their importance in the spiritual and religious experience of the Western World.

OHIO UNIVERSITY LIBRARY

Please return this book as soon as you have finished with it. In order to avoid a fine it must be returned by the latest date stamped below.

MAR 9 1975

MAR 7 1975

OCT 22 1994
RETURN BY

OCT 6 1981

OCT 30 1981

MAR 10 1995

RETURN BY

FEB 24 1995

JUN 13 1988

RETURN BY

JUN 13 1988

JAN 18 2007

MAY 31 1989

JUN 13 1993

Quarter Loan

MAY 9 1993

SEP 7 1994

QUARTER LOAN

JAN 3 1995

QUARTER LOAN

CF